Gender and Society in the New Guinea Highlands

WOMEN IN CROSS-CULTURAL PERSPECTIVE

Sue-Ellen Jacobs
University of Washington,
Series Editor

About the Book and Author

The societies of the New Guinea Highlands are among the last-contacted horticulturalist peoples of the world. Endemic warfare, elaborate systems of exchange, flamboyant personality styles, and exaggerated forms of antagonism between the sexes have made them a subject of interest to anthropologists for three decades. This book examines the relationship between the sexes, especially the attitudes and behavior of men toward women, as a result of the economic, political, and structural constraints of Highland social organization. Hostility toward women, which is evident in a high level of violence toward women and an articulated fear of association with them, is given special attention.

Dr. Gelber's study is unique not only because it treats gender relations in the entire culture area of the Highlands, but also because a broad array of types of anthropological analysis—ecosystemic, population-regulatory, economic, sociopolitical, psychological, and ideational—are considered for their relevance to the phenomenon of intersexual hostility. The author's emphasis on underlying problems of explanation and theory, as well as the treatment of attitudes and beliefs as a function of socioeconomic constraints, is a departure from previous modes of analysis and raises new issues in anthropological theory and in the study of gender.

Marilyn G. Gelber received a Ph.D. from Harvard University and has worked as a consultant anthropologist for the World Bank.

Gender and Society in the New Guinea Highlands

An Anthropological Perspective on Antagonism Toward Women

Marilyn G. Gelber

Westview Press / Boulder and London

Women in Cross-Cultural Perspective

This Westview softcover edition is printed on acid-free paper and bound in softcovers that carry the highest rating of the National Association of State Textbook Administrators, in consultation with the Association of American Publishers and the Book Manufacturers' Institute.

Epigraph on p. 93 from T. S. Eliot, "Sweeney Agonistes," *Collected Poems 1909–1962*, copyright 1936 by Harcourt Brace Jovanovich, Inc., and renewed 1963 and 1964 by T. S. Eliot. Reprinted by permission of the publishers, Harcourt Brace Jovanovich, Inc., and Faber and Faber Limited, London.

All photographs were taken by Gary Gelber.

All rights reserved. No part of this publication may be reproduced or transmitted in any form or by any means, electronic or mechanical, including photocopy, recording, or any information storage and retrieval system, without permission in writing from the publisher.

Copyright © 1986 by Westview Press, Inc.

Published in 1986 in the United States of America by Westview Press, Inc.; Frederick A. Praeger, Publisher; 5500 Central Avenue, Boulder, Colorado 80301

Library of Congress Cataloging-in-Publication Data
Gelber, Marilyn G.
  Gender and society in the New Guinea Highlands.
  (Women in cross-cultural perspective)
  Bibliography: p.
  Includes index.
  1. Women—Papua New Guinea. 2. Sex role—Papua New Guinea. 3. Interpersonal conflict—Papua New Guinea
  4. Papua New Guinea—Social life and customs.
  5. Ethnology—Papua New Guinea. I. Title. II. Series
GN671.N5G45 1986   305.4′2′09953   86-11190
ISBN 0-8133-7263-1

Composition for this book was provided by the author.
This book was produced without formal editing by the publisher.

Printed and bound in the United States of America

∞ The paper used in this publication meets the requirements of the American National Standard for Permanence of Paper for Printed Library Materials Z39.48-1984.

6   5   4   3   2   1

In memory of my grandmother,
Celia Marienstrauss Propper.

Contents

Acknowledgments	xi
1. Introduction	1
2. Ideology About Women as a Form of Gerontocratic Control	17
3. The Social Matrix of the Relationship Between the Sexes	47
4. Socio-Economic Structure and Personality	63
5. Aversion Toward Women as a Population Regulatory Device	93
6. Aversion Toward Women as a Population Regulatory Device, II: Problems in Explanation	115
7. Conclusion	149
Bibliography	159
Index	177

Acknowledgments

For their assistance with unpublished data, I would like to thank Bruce Taylor, Patsy Klaus, and Anita Timrots of the Bureau of Justice Statistics, U.S. Department of Justice.

Sections of the book were benefited by discussion with Leo Goldenberg, Gary Gelber, and Abraham Elterman. I am grateful to them for their comments.

If Roger Wallace had not pushed me into the computer age, I would probably still be retyping the manuscript. I thank him for his friendship, his moral support, and his technical assistance.

For the latest in computer technology, and for his unfailing graciousness and good humor, I am deeply grateful to Clyde Steiner. Micheline Meneau and Christophe Meneau kindly shared their expertise in graphics software.

Of the dozens of things for which I am grateful to my husband, Gary Gelber, I thank him especially for the photographs which appear in this book, for his generosity, and for listening to the inner music.

Marilyn G. Gelber

" ... *either for tragedy, comedy, history, pastoral, pastoral-comical, historical-pastoral, tragical-historical, tragical-comical-historical-pastoral ...* "
Polonius, *Hamlet*, Act II, Scene II

1

Introduction

I

"If a young woman offers you food and you eat it, your skin will become no good. You must not eat from such a woman; her hand is taboo." "If you meet a young woman, do not look at her face; if you look at her and she looks at you, then you will copulate. If you do this, something will come up all over your skin, your body will be spoilt. Hear what we say."
Warrior leader of the lineage, Fore tribe, Eastern Highlands, speaking to male novices undergoing initiation (1).

What gives rise to attitudes such as those expressed by the lineage leader of the Fore tribe? How can we explain their existence, and their relationship to the economic and social organization of Highland societies? And of what do the explanations themselves consist? These three questions form the structure of an inquiry into the relationship between the sexes in the New Guinea Highlands.

II

"Men [of the Mae Enga, Western Highlands] believe that the vital fluid residing in a man's skin makes it sound and handsome, a condition that determines and reflects his mental vigor and self-confidence. This fluid also manifests itself as his semen. Hence, every ejaculation depletes his vitality, and over-indulgence must dull his mind and leave his body permanently exhausted and withered" (2).
Meggitt, "Male-Female Relationships in the Highlands of Australian New Guinea."

"Have you ever loved a woman ... physically loved her? There's a feeling of loss, a profound sense of emptiness. Luckily, I was able to interpret the signs correctly. It was a loss of essence ... Women sense my power, and they seek me out ... But I deny them my life essence" (3). "God willing, we shall prevail in peace and freedom from fear and in true health through the purity and essence of our natural fluids" (4).
General Jack Ripper, *Dr. Strangelove, or, How I Learned to Stop Worrying and Love the Bomb.*

The relationship between men and women is complex in every part of the world. As a set of structured relations between two groups of people in a society, it has a special character unlike any other, combining in one relationship economic, social structural, political, reproductive, psychological and ideational elements.

In the New Guinea Highlands, many of the structural and interpersonal tensions which characterize the relationship between the sexes in American society and in other societies present themselves in an exaggerated form. The Highlanders of New Guinea hold up not a mirror, but nearly a caricature of certain aspects of our own society, and probably for this reason, they have been a source of great fascination to anthropologists for several decades (5).

Fear and disgust toward women, an intense interest in the body and its products, sometimes disguised by phobias, and a feeling that men and women are so different as to be almost two different species – these attitudes exist in a milder and more repressed way in American society, but pervade Highland society in an explicit, almost flamboyant,

Introduction

form. Violence toward women is a commonplace both in Highland society and in our own (6), but is met with fewer sanctions in the Highlands.

Although we may see certain similarities between the New Guinea Highlands and American society, it is not an easy task to explain the existence of these attitudes in either case. The relationship between the sexes is interwoven into a complex reticulation of other socio-economic and political structures and processes in both Highland society and our own.

The New Guinea Highlands area is an especially apt region in which to study the relationship between men and women, its causes, and the way it is enmeshed with other aspects of the socio-economic system. Because the Highlands have distinct geographical boundaries, were contacted by the West only since World War II, and make use of relatively simple technology, it is reasonable to treat the various aspects of ecological, economic, and social organization as an articulated set of relationships within a defined system. It is certainly simpler than trying to do the same for American society, if we were attempting to explain the relationship between the sexes there. But some of the causal linkages and types of processes we uncover in a simpler society may be useful to the understanding of sex roles in our own society as well.

An exceptionally large literature concerning sex roles, economy, and socio-political structure in the Highlands also provides an excellent source of description, seen from various points of view.

The Highlands are of great interest to the study of anthropological theory for another reason: the phenomenon of the relationship between the sexes has been explained, in part, by using nearly every major type of anthropological theory (7). By "type of theory" I refer to those causal factors which are given the most weight in the explanation, although very often the theory itself is not made explicit in the argument, and problematical aspects of the theory may be accepted as given. Explanations have been offered in terms of ecological relations, population regulation, economy, social structure, warfare, psychology, and belief system, and sometimes in combinations of these. Like Polonius, we can find ourselves speaking of the techno-environmental, socio-economic, ideational-psychological, ecological-materialist –

and so forth - as we grapple with the multiple and interlocking causes of behavior and belief.

All of these perspectives are worthy, but each of the explanations taken by itself does not account for significant aspects of the problem. Anthropological explanations are notably difficult to give, hampered by the lack of a well-defined and generally accepted body of laws and a hierarchy of causal relations, such as those common in the physical sciences (8).

Because the Highlands area is so well described, it represents an almost unique test case for the various theories and for bringing to light certain problems which the theories themselves present.

There are two concurrent areas of inquiry in this study, then: the explanation of antagonism toward women in the Highlands, and a look at the problems implicit in some of the explanatory suggestions themselves.

In particular, I will examine some aspects of the theory underlying explanation in ecological and population regulatory terms, and in psychological terms. In attempting to extricate some of the tacit assumptions of these theories, I do not mean to suggest that the theories, or the explanations which they support, are invalid or lacking in usefulness. Rather, I am trying to exemplify the problems sometimes posed by anthropological explanation, when the terms in which the explanation is given are themselves in need of clarification, and when a structure of relations in the theory needs to be brought to light, which would order the meanings of the terms with respect to one another.

Perhaps it is superfluous to say that our understanding of a subject is dependent on description (itself based on an implicit theory of what is important and needs mentioning) and on explanation. By making the theory underlying an explanation clearer and more explicit in its own right, the explanation can be strengthened, and our understanding of the subject obviously enlarged. It is for this reason that some of the major theories which have been used to explain the relationship between men and women in the Highlands are the focus of attention in the present study, as well as the relationship between men and women itself.

The fundamental problem in explaining the nature of the relationship between men and women in the New Guinea

Highlands is that antagonism between the sexes is mostly describable as a psychological or ideational problem (with behavioral ramifications, of course), and yet its explanation cannot be given only with reference to psychological causes, or in terms of its "fit" with other aspects of a conceptual scheme. Factors stemming from the economic and sociopolitical organization of Highland society, as well perhaps as from the overall adaptation of the society to its environment, must be taken into account in explaining these attitudes and beliefs. One of the most important questions, and one which is very difficult to answer, is how these various types of phenomena – psychological, economic, political, and so forth – are to be linked in a causal sequence, or set of interlocking sequences. It is probable that a direct linear chain of causality will not do justice to the complex interactions among them.

III

The societies of the New Guinea Highlands, with a total population of approximately 750,000, lie between 4500 and 8000 feet in altitude, in the Central Cordillera of New Guinea, one of the largest islands in the world.

Although the Highlands resemble other parts of Melanesia in certain respects, such as leadership by big men and the importance of ceremonial exchange, and have features in common with Coastal and Sepik New Guinea, such as rituals which express a strong dichotomy between the sexes, they have usually been treated as a discrete area for study.

According to Brookfield, a geographer, the cultivation practices of the Highlanders are "at all points ... readily distinguishable from their lowland neighbors" in terms of "much greater elaboration of land preparation, crop rotation, inter-cropping, and special techniques" (9). The agricultural region may be "precisely defined" by the methods of control of water, soil nutrients, and soil erosion (10), which allow a much more productive use of land than the employment of simpler techniques would (11).

Anthropometric and serological studies have shown that the peoples of the Highlands have significant physical and genetic similarities as well (12).

The present study is limited to the Highlands per se, as defined by Brookfield and others (13), and by the features noted below - that is, from the Enga in the west to the Fore in the east (the Mendi and Huli being the southernmost and the Maring the furthest north), as well as some notes on the Kapauku and Dani of Irian Jaya.

Although they are very interesting, groups on the fringe areas of the Highlands and at lower elevations, such as the Sambia, the Etoro, the Kaluli, and the Baruya, are not a part of the present study, since they differ considerably from the Highlands in population density, horticultural practices, staple crop, reliance on hunting, comparative unimportance of pigs, and lack of elaborate exchange, as well as in ritual organization and in their sexual orientation and concerns (14).

The societies of the Highlands, on the other hand, share many characteristics of economic and social structure. Subsistence activities are typified by the intensive horticulture of a single crop, the sweet potato (Ipomoea batatas), the keeping of pigs, and a virtual lack of dependence on wild foods. Specialized horticultural techniques are used in combination, such as tilling, contour planting, terracing, soil fences, ditching, and composting.

Women are responsible for most repetitive horticultural tasks, including planting, weeding, and harvesting, and also for cooking, the care of children and animals, net manufacture, and transportation of food, water, children, and firewood. Men clear the land of large trees, make fences, and employ specialized horticultural techniques. Men's activities are done on a sporadic basis and occupy comparatively little of their time, particularly since the introduction of the steel axe, which occurred prior to the time during which the ethnographic studies were undertaken.

Exchange, ceremonial or through trade, of pigs, pork, and non-utilitarian valuables, culminating in populous feasts in which many pigs are killed, is the most important focus of activity for men. Prestige, gained through the size and scope of display, prestation, and exchange, is an important goal of rivalry and competition, and generally determines the political alignment within the society.

Leaders, called "big men," are in many groups (particularly in the Western Highlands) those who are the most successful in ceremonial exchange. They exercise their power by virtue of consensus and by force of personality, without the support of formalized structures of authority.

Highland societies maintain a patrilineal ideology, but the actual recruitment to local groups takes place through various sources, including affinal and cognatic connections and the efforts of big men to recruit supporters, and through the incorporation of refugees produced by chronic feuding between neighboring groups.

Residence is normally patrivirilocal, and village exogamy is practiced. Nucleated villages are more common in the Eastern Highlands, and dispersed homesteads in the Western Highlands. Men in both regions live in a joint men's house, and women live with their unmarried daughters, young sons, and animals. Polygyny is regarded by men as desirable, but it is not always achieved. Boys are initiated into the men's house during adolescence, and in some groups there are purificatory rituals for bachelors. Rituals concerned with fertility and increase, and specifically excluding women, are also common.

Marriage is one of the major occasions for ceremonial exchange, chiefly in the form of bridewealth payments. Affinal relatives, particularly husband and wife's brother, later may become important trade partners; other people of each locality may subsequently be drawn into trade relations by the original affinal connection. Despite the fact that marriage facilitates exchange, antagonism pervades the relationship between men and women.

Some of the Highland societies are more thoroughly described than others with reference to the various ramifications of antagonism between the sexes; published studies of these societies, including the Melpa, Kuma, and Mae Enga of the Western Highlands, and the Bena Bena, Kamano, Gahuku-Gama, and Gururumba of the Eastern Highlands, provide a large proportion of the information upon which the present study is based. Information is also drawn from studies of the Maring and Chimbu of the Western Highlands, and the Fore and Tairora of the Eastern Highlands, as well as of other Highland societies such as the Kyaka and the Manga of the Western Highlands, the Siane of the Eastern Highlands, and the Huli and Mendi of the Southern Highlands (15).

The mid-1970's marked the independence of Papua New Guinea from Australian administration, and many changes have occurred in the Highlands in the decade since, particularly with respect to labor migration, cash cropping, increased mobility, and in general an increasing integration into a money economy (16). Nearly all of the ethnographic studies which are sources for the present work were undertaken between the middle 1950's and the middle 1970's; the "ethnographic present" refers to that period.

There are of course differences among Highland societies, especially between those of the Eastern and Western Highlands. The Western Highland societies in general have a higher population density (especially the Enga and Chimbu), somewhat more intensified methods of agriculture (17), larger scale and more complex forms of ceremonial exchange (such as the Enga *Te* and the Melpa *Moka*), and a concomitant emphasis on success in competitive exchange as a criterion for the position of big man.

In the Eastern Highlands (as well as in some areas in the outer part of the Highlands, such as the Maring), by contrast, the position of big man may be determined by success in reaching a consensus, by organizational abilities in warfare, or by sheer force of personality. Initiation rites involving bloodletting, and purificatory rituals for young men, are also more common in the Eastern Highlands.

In treating the societies of the Highlands in terms of their shared characteristics, I do not mean to minimize the differences among them. To a reader most familiar with the distinctive traits of any particular Highlands group, a generalization about the Highlands may appear to do an injustice to those traits, and to distort, in an overly presbyopic manner, the internal coherence of a unique societal integration.

But it is at least as distorting to minimize the great preponderance of characteristics which the societies of the Highlands have in common. The focus in the present study is restricted to these generally shared traits, used for both the "independent variable" in the formulation (aspects of economic, social, and political organization) and the "dependent variable" (relations between the sexes, and attitudes toward women).

I do not mean to establish an "ideal type" of Highland society and culture, nor, by focusing on shared characteristics, to suggest that variation is lacking. But the similarities among Highland societies, considerably outweighing the differences, in subsistence practices, economic processes, and socio-political organization on the one hand, and beliefs and behavior concerning relations between the sexes on the other, strongly suggest that a common set of processes link the former and the latter.

It is only by looking at the entire Highlands that certain trends in these processes have emerged. Some isolated data whose importance may be difficult to assess in one society alone assume a different significance when they become part of a correlation, or at least a trend, seen to recur in many or most of the Highland societies.

The alternative point of view, if carried to its logical conclusion, would suggest that the socio-economic, political, and symbolic processes of each society require an explanation separate from that of any other society – something probably few would want to maintain.

It did not seem especially fruitful in the present study to compare the societies of the Highlands in terms of the covariance of the differences among them. The selection of relevant variables for covariance presumes a prior assumption of causal relationships among the variables (or the assumption of a causal relationship of these variables to other factors). But it is these very causal relationships for which I was looking.

Andrew Strathern (18) has discussed in some detail the pronounced difficulty of delimiting, defining, and measuring variables for comparison among Highland societies, as well as the lack of direct comparability among the data for different groups.

These considerations, the unwieldiness of the very large number of relevant axes of covariance which ideally should be taken into account, and the questionable relative importance of the variations themselves, make a comparison among Highland societies a less interesting project, and perhaps a less enlightening one, than a search for the structure and processes, common to all or most Highland societies, which generate antagonism toward women.

A certain amount of antagonism between the sexes, depending on the definition of antagonism, may be a feature of most human societies. Differentiation between the sexes

Table 1.1   Distribution of Characteristics of Antagonism

Eastern Highlands

Trait	Bena[a]	Kamano[b]	Gahuku[c]	Gururumba[d]	Fore[e]	Siane[f]	Tairora[g]
Residential separation/men's house	x	x	x	x	x	x	x*
Male initiation which excludes women	x	x	x	x	x	x	x*
Other male ritual which excludes/devalues women	x	x	x	x	x	x	
Ritual attacks by women against men	x	x	x	x	x		
Physical violence against women	x	x	x	x	x		x
Fear of sexual relations	x	x	x	x	x	x	x
Fear of menstruation or other female pollution	x	x	x	x	x		x
Most of labor done by women	x	x	x	x	x	x	x
Disproportionate female suicide	x	x		x	x		x

*existed prior to reference's fieldwork
Sources: [a]Langness 1967b;1969;1974. [b]Berndt 1962. [c]Read 1952;1954a. [d]Newman 1964a;1965. [e]Lindenbaum 1972;1976; Berndt 1962. [f]Salisbury 1962;1965. [g]Watson 1970.

(Continued)

Table 1.1, (Cont.) Distribution of Characteristics of Antagonism

Western, Central, and Southern Highlands

Trait	Mae-Enga[h]	Chimbu[i]	Melpa[j]	Maring[k]	Kyaka[l]	Huli[m]	Kuma[n]
Residential separation/ men's house	x	x	x	x	x	x	x
Male initiation which excludes women	x	x*	none		x	x	x
Other male ritual which excludes/devalues women	x	x*	x	x	x	x	x
Ritual attacks by women against men	x verbal	x	x				x
Physical violence against women	x		x	x*	x	x	x
Fear of sexual relations	x	x	x	x		x	
Fear of menstruation or other female pollution	x	x	x	x	x	x	x
Most of labor done by women	x	x	x	x	x	possibly not	x
Disproportionate female suicide		x	x	x	x	x	x

*existed prior to reference's fieldwork
Sources: [h]Meggitt 1964;1965a;1976. [i]Brown 1964;1969;1972. [j]M. Strathern 1972. [k]Buchbinder and Rappaport 1976; Rappaport 1968;1969. Lowman-Vayda 1968; [l]Bulmer 1960;1965;1971. [m]Glasse 1965;1968;1974. [n]Reay 1959a;1959b.

of normative personality characteristics, some division of labor, and a shared sense among each sex of differing from the opposite sex, for example, probably are typical of most societies. In the New Guinea Highlands, however, antagonism between the sexes, particularly on the part of men toward women, is a prominent and pervasive feature of the social structure.

Among the most obvious aspects of antagonism (19) in the Highlands are residential separation, men's houses, men's secret ritual (part of the explicit intent of which is to exclude and devalue women), physical violence toward women, including rape, murder, and attacks upon their genitals, the exploitation of the surplus value of women's labor, expressed ideology concerning fear of women's exuviae, including menstrual blood, and of sexual relations with women, disparagement by men of women and their activities, and ritualized and ineffectual attacks by women on men. The distribution of these characteristics is shown in Table 1.1 (20).

Other important aspects of the antagonistic relationship between the sexes include struggles between the sexes over the allocation of goods, the exclusion of women from political and ritual activity, the coercion of women into marriages which they do not want, the lack of freedom of movement for women, and the disproportionate rate of suicide among Highlands women.

Still other aspects include the "dimorphism" between the sexes of normative personality characteristics, the integration of negative beliefs about women, pollution, and sexual relations into a system of other beliefs, and sentiments, conscious or unconscious, about relations between the sexes expressed in ritual and myth. With hard work, it is possible to deduce a little about unconscious emotions from the descriptions of hysterical psychoses, dreams, jokes, and taunts.

Most of the manifestations of antagonism between the sexes appear to be on the part of men toward women rather than the reverse. It is possible that this in itself may be an indication of antagonism and the resulting status of women; that is, because of their relative lack of power, women may be afraid to express their hostile sentiments about men openly, and certainly they have fewer opportunities to act upon their sentiments.

Introduction

It is also possible that the data on women's sentiments may be under-reported in the literature on the Highlands, which suffers in a number of ways from characterizations of women's behavior stereotypic to our own society (21). The notions of women's "gossip" (22), "squabbles" (23), "nagging" (24), "complaints" (25), "running home" (26), and "chatter" (27), appear tacitly to reflect the ways in which women in our own society were traditionally described. It is possible as well that women do not maintain the same type or degree of hostility toward men as the reverse, or that the hostility is not as well articulated. Women as a group do not appear to have a dogmatized ideology regarding men as a group (28).

For these reasons, it is primarily the antagonism of men toward women which is the subject of my investigation. But antagonism must be seen in the total context of the relationship between men and women, and the relationship between the sexes must in turn be seen in the context of the economic and social structure of which it is a part. Antagonism, in terms of emotion, may refer to fear, hostility, avoidance, deprecation, revulsion, and envy, and other related sentiments. We need to ask: where do these attitudes come from?

Notes - Chapter One

1. R. Berndt 1962:103.
2. Meggitt 1964:210.
3. P. George and Stanley Kubrick 1963:81.
4. ibid:38.
5. Allen 1967; C. Berndt 1966; R. Berndt 1962; Biersack 1984; Brown 1964; 1969; Brown and Buchbinder 1976; Buchbinder and Rappaport 1976; Faithorn 1975; 1976; Feil 1978b; Gillison 1980; Glasse 1968; 1974; n.d.; Herdt and Poole 1982; Josephides 1983; 1985; Langness 1967a; 1967b; 1974; 1976; Lindenbaum 1972; 1976; LiPuma 1978; Meggitt 1964; 1976; Meigs 1978; 1984; Newman 1965; O'Brien 1984; Read 1952; 1954a; 1954b; 1982; Reay 1959a; 1959b; Rubel and Rosman 1978; Ryan 1969; Sexton 1984; A. Strathern 1969a; 1970b; 1979; M. Strathern 1972; 1978; 1980; 1981; 1984; Walter 1978; and others.
6. According to the Bureau of Justice Statistics, U.S. Department of Justice (personal communication), 2,323,534 women in the United States were victims of violent crime in 1984: 164,480

raped, 400,770 robbed, 1,754,070 assaulted, and 4,214 murdered (90% of the murders were committed by men). The majority of victims were beween the ages of 16 and 34. We are very far from understanding the reasons.

7. Several types of anthropological theory, and some of the problems associated with them, are distinguished by Kaplan and Manners (1972).

8. According to Nagel (1961:47-52), a general law has the form, "if $\underline{x}$ is A, then $\underline{x}$ is B." Moreover, it will support a "subjunctive conditional" or "contra-factual," i.e., can be stated, "for any $\underline{x}$, if $\underline{x}$ were A, then $\underline{x}$ would be B," thus making possible prediction as well as explanation; to explain a phenomenon is to subsume it as a particular case of a general law.

The question of the possibility of prediction in anthropology, and hence of the status of prediction as a requirement for law-like statements, deserves extensive examination elsewhere.

9. Brookfield 1961:437.

10. Brookfield 1962:248.

11. Brookfield distinguishes two sets of Highlands groups which make use of these specialized techniques: one between the Wissel Lakes and the Baliem Valley, in West Irian, and the other between the Huli and the Kainantu shelf, in Papua New Guinea (1964:20). He excludes the Telefolmin and Ok Sibil (Star Mountains) groups as well as "the peoples on the outer slopes of the Cordillera of New Guinea" (ibid.). He also notes that the Dani, in West Irian, are more closely related linguistically to the Highlands groups in Papua New Guinea than the Telefolmin people are (who are located between the Dani and the PNG Highlands).

12. Bulmer and Bulmer 1964.

13. Brown 1978:267.

14. Schieffelin 1976; Kelly 1977:7-18; Godelier 1982:6 ff.; Herdt 1984:56 ff.

15. I visited the Fore, Kuma, Chimbu, Melpa, Wiru, and Mendi peoples of the Highlands in the summer of 1977.

16. eg., A. Strathern 1979; Read 1982; Rappaport 1984.

17. Feil (1986) suggests that higher average rainfall in the Western Highlands may have supported intensified horticulture of taro in some areas dating to 2500-2000 B.P., and that the greater elaboration of exchange and of intensified sweet potato production in the present day Western Highlands may have been a historical evolution from earlier forms of intensified cultivation, which were absent in the the Eastern Highlands.

18. A. Strathern 1969a:49-51. Galton's problem may also hamper comparison.

19. Herdt and Poole (1982:4,21) point out that the term "sexual antagonism" (which I have in general not used) has "covered" (ibid.) a great number of topics (which I would summarize as various aspects of social organization, belief system, and psychological

Introduction

development and experience), without sufficient distinctions having been drawn among the usages. I have tried to avoid such undesirable vagueness by specifying, as below in the text, just which are the aspects of antagonism to which I refer, both in description and in method of analysis.

20. Blank data points indicate a lack of data.

21. O'Brien (1984) discusses the misrepresentation of women's activities and beliefs in studies of the Highlands, as well as of other areas in Melanesia.

22. Meggitt 1964:216; Heider 1970:190.
23. Langness 1967b:171.
24. ibid.
25. Rappaport 1968:159; Modjeska 1982:83-84.
26. M. Strathern 1972:258.
27. M. Strathern 1978:181.
28. ibid:146,152; M. Strathern 1981:179,185.

"Mais comment est-il arrivé qu'un acte dont le but est si solennel, et auquel la nature nous invite par l'attrait le plus puissant ... soit devenu la source la plus féconde de notre dépravation et de nos maux?
... C'est par la tyrannie de l'homme, qui a converti la possession de la femme en une propriété.
Par les moeurs et les usages, qui ont surchargé de conditions l'union conjugale" (1).
Diderot, *Supplement au Voyage de Bougainville*, 1772

2

Ideology About Women as a Form of Gerontocratic Control

I

"[A boy] is taught that his whole development may be jeopardized if he does not exercise extreme care in his relations with the opposite sex, and he is permitted only a minimum of contact with the women of the community. He eats only foodstuffs which have been cooked by men and he is not permitted to sleep in the women's houses. He is, moreover, warned of the danger to himself if he succumbs to the blandishments of women ... his strength may be impaired by contact with them ... women are believed to be the principal agents for sorcerers" (2).
"Boys are repeatedly cautioned not to spend too much time with women; if they do, 'their skins will be no good,' 'their work will go wrong,' 'they will die young,' and so on" (3).

In this sort of way, the older men of the Highlands villages instruct young men to avoid contact with women. Young men are repeatedly warned to avoid the repellant and polluting dangers of association with women, sometimes in ritual contexts and at other times informally (4).

Yet older men themselves seem to fear the pollutive dangers of women much less than they exhort younger men to do. There appears to be a marked difference between the beliefs and behavior of older men and of younger men. A rather large number of authors have noted in passing that a more relaxed association is permitted with women in later years (5), or that older men are not as anxious about the dangers associated with sexual relations (6). The reasons for this discrepancy have not previously been dealt with in a systematic way, however.

The disparity between what older men say and what they themselves do can be quite striking. Although the New Guinea Highlands are well known for the prevalent set of beliefs concerning the danger of association with women, it seems that this ideology is not adhered to equally by all subgroups of the society.

There may be more than one version of an organized system of belief even in a society relatively undifferentiated in technological specialization and division of labor. To speak of "the ideology" of "the society" may obscure the differences in the various collective representations of reality of different societal groups, distinguished by age, sex, ritual specialization, or other factors. The uses to which ideology, or organized sets of beliefs held up as norms, may be put, may also be obscured by assuming that a unique ideology is espoused by all (7).

In the New Guinea Highlands, we need to ask why older men and younger men appear to believe and act differently from one another, and why the older men encourage the younger men to adopt sentiments which they themselves apparently do not feel strongly.

There is quite a bit of evidence that the sentiments of younger men toward women are heavily influenced by older men. The fact that older men repeatedly warn the younger men and boys about the repellent dangers of women has been very frequently reported (8). Newman, for example, notes the following: "As they [boys undergoing initiation] perspire [from being made to sit next to a fire], quantities of dirt and grease are removed by scraping their skins with sticks. This filth is said to be the product of living with women, and they are told that their bodies will never grow strong if they continue associating with women for they will be forever accumulating debilitating dirt" (9).

The contrast between the self-restraint enjoined upon the younger generation and the florid sexuality of the older generation can at times be quite striking. For example, in the courting parties of Siane young people (10), physical contact between a young man and a young woman is limited to swaying in unison with their noses touching and sleeping, in a literal sense, jointly. At the same moment, the adults of the locality are engaged in watching sexual farces involving "the grossest caricatures" (11), considered hilarious, during which the actors pretend to attempt sodomy with members of the audience.

As we have seen, older men are considerably less anxious about the dangers of association with women; in at least some, if not all groups, they may actively and sometimes even in a lecherous manner seek out and enjoy sexual relations (12).

There is also the obvious fact that procreation must occur in order for the society to replace itself efficiently. This is recognized by the Highlands men themselves; older men show great interest in procreation, often in the interests of strengthening the local group, and may even feel that women are deliberately denying them desired children (13). The older men in some cases put younger men in a kind of double-bind by urging them to get married and have children while simultaneously warning them to avoid women (14).

Why should the attitudes expressed to younger men by older men differ so much from their own behavior? One important reason is that older and younger men are potentially competitors for women.

Women are the major source of productive labor in Highland societies; their contribution to production outweighs by far the contribution of men (15). The responsibilities of women include clearing underbrush, planting, tending, harvesting and transporting the staple root crop and other vegetables, raising and caring for pigs, transporting water and firewood, cooking, manufacturing net bags and clothing, and caring for children.

The contribution of men to production is seasonal and is limited to clearing the land of large trees, constructing fences, and in some cases raising a few minor crops, usually in tree form, which require little tending. Men spend most of their time realigning themselves politically and arranging matters concerning ceremonial exchange, the basis of which are pigs produced by women. Men probably spent more time in subsistence work prior to the introduction of the steel axe (16), but this occurred well before any of the ethnographic studies were undertaken.

Although women's labor is disparaged by men as drudgery (17), men recognize their economic dependence on women (18). Several aphorisms used by men in the Highlands express a consciousness on the part of men that women's labor is used to their advantage. "'Women are our tractors'" (19), in the view of Bena Bena men; the male Melpa say that "'women are like tradestores'" (20). Fore men say that "'wives do all the hard work, they are the hands of men'" (21). Regarding the arrangement of marriages and the resulting exchange of valuables, the older Bena men assert that "'it is our business'" (22); similarly, although not expressed epigrammatically, the Manga, according to Cook, " ... are quick to forestall elopements because marriageable girls represent a capital asset to the clan" (23).

Political success, the achievement of the position of big man, is in many Highland societies dependent upon success in ceremonial exchange, which is in turn dependent upon the production of pigs. Pigs have a uniquely important role in exchange, as the most highly valued items of trade.

Several other goods, such as shells of various sorts, are also traded, usually in exchange for pigs. Of these, only salt, a comparatively minor item traded prior to the introduction of Western salt, had a utilitarian purpose. The role of "prestige goods" in technologically unsophisticated economies has received considerable discussion in the theoretical literature of economic anthropology (24). Many suggestions have been made about what it is that "prestige goods" represent, including surplus, wealth, a way of saving or investing, a quantity convertible to subsistence goods, or a means of political control.

Rappaport has suggested that "prestige goods" in the economy of the New Guinea Highlands "stimulated the production and facilitated the distribution of the utilitarian goods" (25). If there were no non-utilitarian goods in circulation, according to this argument, the production of utilitarian goods would be determined only by the demand for the commodity for which they were exchanged; i.e., only enough salt would be produced by salt producers to satisfy their need for the axes they received in exchange for salt. The demand for any one utilitarian good is also limited, and "if only salt and stone axes could be exchanged for each other, the maintenance of a supply of both throughout the population would require a balance between the quantities of each produced and between their respective exchange values, both of which constantly fluctuate in response to such processes as local demographic changes" (26).

Pigs play an interesting role in exchange, because they are both prestige items and utilitarian items, and because their value as either can be controlled in part by what is done with them. They may be traded in living form, or on a very temporary basis as pork, or they may be consumed as pork. Consequently, potential inflation of the numbers of pigs (and the attendant devaluation of their worth as exchange items) can be controlled by consumption in its most literal sense - by removing the pigs from circulation and eating them.

Pigs, because they are crucial to ceremonial exchange, are subject to very great demand. Because they are produced entirely by women, more specifically by wives, the demand for the labor of women is also very great (27). The demand for the labor of women is facilitated by, and probably responsible for, the possibility of polygynous marriage in the Highlands (28). At the same time, the pressure of demand for women causes scarcity of supply. The number of wives a man may have does not seem to have a well-defined upper limit. A big man among the Tairora, for example, is reported to have had twenty wives (29); another, among the Huli, had twenty-one wives (30).

Consequently, it seems very likely that those who have achieved control over the source of scarce productive labor, namely polygynously married older men, will seek both to retain control and to augment their relative power by increasing the amount of production which they control.

Retaining and augmenting power through the control of production are particularly important in the Highlands because there is constant competition for prestige and political power, which in most Highland societies is gained primarily through economic success. At the same time, the hold of an individual man on political power is tenuous, and not reinforced by formal institutions of authority. Retaining power is therefore crucially dependent on continuing control over the production and distribution of pigs.

Apart from the scarcity created by the demand for women's labor (and the associated polygyny), there may be some other, less significant, reasons for the scarcity of women as well. However, female infanticide (as well as male infanticide) appears to have been rare (31), and consequently not a significant cause of scarcity. Of the four groups for which it was reported, it was no longer practised by two (32) at the time of ethnographic study, and exact data are not available. In the third group, "there is no discrimination according to the baby's sex" (33). In the fourth group, the paternal grandmother might intervene to save the child, and female infanticide is represented in a pedagogical tale as leading to "incest, patricide, and confusion" (34). Bowers, a demographer, found no evidence of female infanticide among the Kakoli of the Western Highlands (35); from a sample of 1166 births, 40% more male children than female children died in the first year of life (95 vs. 68). These figures certainly do not indicate preferential neglect of female children, considered by demographers to be an important form of infanticide.

In some groups, differential mortality rates for adult men and women may result in a disproportionately large number of men (36). Wealthier Highland societies may also be able to obtain a disproportionate number of wives from less wealthy societies, leaving the latter with a shortage of women.

That women are scarce is indicated by a number of other factors. Several authors have reported the existence of permanent bachelorhood (37). The fact that older men are married to younger women, and that female children may be married or betrothed (38), suggests that the supply of women of the same age as the potential young husband has been exhausted, as wives of the previous generation or half-generation.

Younger women may be more desirable as wives for several reasons. It is possible that they are stronger and more efficient workers, although information on this subject is lacking. Because of the age differential itself and because of their lack of experience, they may also be more docile as wives. They may be more attractive as sexual partners. (Here we have to leave aside the presumption, stemming from our own society and culture, that this is obvious.) For example, among the Chimbu, subcutaneous fat is considered to be a sign of beauty (39), and in the same group, as well as in others, younger women tend to be considerably fatter than older ones (40). The loss of subcutaneous fat with increasing age is much more pronounced in women than in men in the Highlands (41) and may be due to the differential expenditure of energy in production, to dietary insufficiencies, which may differ between men and women, or to the stress of childbearing and lactation in the presence of the first two factors.

This conjunction of an aesthetic judgment with a scarce and depreciating good suggests that there may be some relationship between what is considered beautiful in women and the socio-economic significance of the aspects of beauty; the subject was touched upon by Veblen (42) long ago.

I have been arguing that older men foster the sentiments of fear and revulsion toward women in younger men, and that this serves to some degree to remove younger men from competition with older men for women. At the same stage of life at which these exhortations are made, younger men and adolescents often in fact do remove themselves from their natal village (43), sometimes for a period of years. In other cases, adolescents and young unmarried men may remain, but they voluntarily avoid women in their own village (44).

In saying that young men avoid women "voluntarily," we should keep in mind that their volition is relative to the values in which they have been previously inculcated. For example, among the Etoro, who are located slightly outside the Highlands as defined in the strict sense by Brookfield (see Introduction), the ideology regarding sexual relations is such that anyone who does not conform to the pattern most beneficial to older men is thereby committing a supernaturally life-threatening offense (45).

Women are also to some degree controlled by ideology (46), in this case concerning their personality characteristics. M. Strathern has shown that the derogatory stereotypes of women held by the Melpa men are "internally inconsistent" and " ... can be related to certain requirements made of women's roles" (47). Women are characterized as "soft-brained" (48) on the one hand, and as "hard headed" (49) on the other; Strathern relates the first stereotype to the position of women as intermediaries between their husbands and brothers, and their consequent divided loyalties; she relates the second stereotype to the refusal of women to consider only the interests of the husbands' group (50). Similarly, free will seems to be attributed to women (51); I suggest that this is done so that they can be held responsible for their actions (52). Nonetheless, they are given little latitude for the expression of their "free will." Contradictory stereotypes, which are also used to characterize members of minority groups in American society, probably represent an attempt on the part of the more powerful to maintain the behavior of the less powerful group within certain limits.

We have been talking about antagonism in the form of fear of women and revulsion toward them. Antagonism also takes the form of hostility and attempt to control, in certain cases. Antagonism between husband and wife seems to focus in many cases on disputes about control over production and what is to be done with the goods produced (53). For example, a wife may want her husband to trade the pigs she has raised with her own brother, although the husband wishes to use those pigs to acquire another wife.

Interestingly, where sisters provide productive labor for brothers, the relationship between sisters and brothers is also one of hostility (54), although elsewhere it is harmonious.

It is quite obvious that the contribution to production of women in the New Guinea Highlands far outweighs the benefit of consumption which they receive from it. This consumption could be measured in tangible ways, for example, intake of pork (55), amassing of valuables, or amount of leisure time, or in less tangible ways, such as deference, prestige, or power resulting from the production or distribution of goods.

Although women are the producers of goods, they have neither the right of usufruct nor usually of alienation of the most important good produced, that is, pigs (56). Their part in the distribution of nonvegetable goods is minimal. Yet they are at the same time intimately connected, as mothers, wives, sisters, daughters, etc., to those who benefit from their disproportionate contribution to production. They are not simply members of another class, or race, of workers, as they might be in a society technologically more advanced and more differentiated in division of labor.

As intimates, men might find it harder to isolate the difficult life situation of women as belonging to beings quite different from themselves, of whom they have little first-hand knowledge (as with another class or race), without a strong ideology that women *are* beings of some radically different kind than men.

Of course this argument takes as its presumption that people have a need to consider those whom they exploit as alien in some way to themselves. Certainly, disparagement of the personality characteristics of individuals whose contribution to production is disproportionately large, whose consumption is disproportionately small, and whose work is regarded as onerous and repetitive, seems to be a commonplace in many societies. The work is drudgerous; the person who does it becomes at best, in the eyes of others, a drudge.

Women in the Highlands are controlled by ideology, and also to a great degree by physical violence directed against them (57). Brutality toward women can be extreme and is not a rare occurrence. Rape and gang rape, undertaken either in a spirit of "fun" or of retaliation and control, or sometimes gratuitously, are commonplaces in the Highlands. An angry man may focus his attack on a woman by cutting, burning, or otherwise mutilating her genital and reproductive organs (58); often these attacks result in the woman's death. These acts occur with such frequency as to indicate a cultural pattern, not simply the isolated excesses of a psychotic, as perhaps in our own society.

Most of these acts on the part of men are not met with social sanctions from their own local group. Even the murder of a wife may not be treated by other men of the locality as a serious offense. Because of virilocality, married women are most often without local partisans from their own natal groups. Women very often commit suicide, in numbers very disproportionate to those of men, probably because they are driven to it by the untenable nature of their lives (59).

In a group in the Chimbu area which I visited, a man had recently murdered his wife with an axe. He was jailed for it by the authorities, but men from his own locality paid a large sum of money (K300 - about U.S. $425) to have him released "because we felt sorry for him." They were in the process of assembling an indemnity payment to the wife's village when I arrived, and they were preparing to fight a spear battle with her village over a disagreement in the appropriate settlement. Apparently only the woman's mother, who lived in the other village, expressed dissatisfaction with the means, as opposed to the amount, of settlement, saying that nothing would bring her daughter back.

II

We might ask why ideology rather than something else should be used as a significant form of control over the actions of younger men in New Guinea Highland societies, and, assuming that it is, why the particular ideology used to facilitate control should be one regarding women.

Control over the actions of others by influencing their sentiments seems to be a prominent form of social control in the Highlands. This is due to a number of factors specific to Highland social structure, most of which pertain to the lack of structural constraints on individual behavior. In the subsequent chapters, we will see the way in which formal institutions of authority and means of third party adjudication are lacking. In addition, there is an on-going fluctuation in the membership of the local group, with attendant changes of loyalty and enmity, and there are shifting units of sentiment and action for other purposes, such as alignment in support of big men or for ceremonial exchange. There is a constant potential for arrogation of power away from the existing leader; the potential for fission in the group adds to the instability of the situation.

Temporary structural alignments and alliances for any purpose appear to be the result of individual choices and activities, and they are undertaken on an opportunistic basis. Significantly, the importance of the individual's actions in determining structural arrangements (rather than the pre-existence of structural arrangements which would determine the individual's actions) seems to mean that the group structure does not itself act as a unifying force to minimize conflict and to maintain behavior within certain limits. Several authors have noted that social constraints on behavior are minimal (60); as a force which guides behavior, individualism may outweigh even the good of the patrilineage (61). As we will see in a subsequent chapter, political success may result from anti-social behavior, rather than from adherence to norms or to their expression as ideals.

There are few corporate structures or ideological commitments which maintain the unity of the local group and mitigate conflict within it, with the possible exception of patrilineality, which is semi-fictive, and the men's house. There are few, if any, other comparatively permanent structural alliances not based on personal preference, which might otherwise serve to set some limits on behavior. For example, boys initiated at the same time do not form an age set which has a sense of coherent identity or which acts as a group later in life, and age sets are apparently of no special importance to the society's conception of itself.

Similarly, there are no ceremonial organizations, such as moieties, whose membership is relatively permanent and which form part of the society's characterization of itself, and thus might serve as a kind of higher ideal which could guide behavior.

The Highlanders appear to be rather uninterested in the elaboration of a coherent cosmological system and of man's place within it, to which appeal might otherwise be made in the interests of social control. Similarly, there seems to be little poetic vision of human nature or of how people should be, which might otherwise serve as a standard for behavior.

Lawrence and Meggitt (62) have noted that in Melanesian religion "the realm of the non-empirical is always closely associated with, in most cases part of, the empirical world." Propitiation, for economic gain to the living (63), of the ghosts of close relatives and other ancestors, is one of the major elements of Highlands' religion. Reay has characterized the religion of the Kuma as "one of fear and the propitiation of evil" with "no place for positive sentiments or forces for good in the extra-sensory sphere" (64), and she also notes that "concern for the general good informs Kuma materialism with no ascetic or stoic ideal" (65).

The propitiated ghosts are at best undependable and may be vicious, deliberately inflicting harm on their living offspring or siblings. Perhaps they may represent an inchoate metaphor for human nature. Another unschematized metaphor is that of the wild pig (66). Reay notes that the Kuma "say that they would like to be 'like wild pigs,' undisciplined and self-seeking" (67); the Gururumba "compared themselves with pigs that must be watched lest they eat their own offspring" (68).

The complex of structural and other factors outlined above indicates that there are few structural constraints on the behavior of individuals; moreover, the individual is apparently not constrained by rules, or by the expectations of others that he will follow the rules, to as great a degree as in many societies. At the same time, *force majeur*, or physical violence, such as that used to control women, is not an alternative means of effecting control within the local group of men, because it is potentially too disruptive, and because all men have equal access to weapons and are more or less equally strong physically.

Individuals in Highland societies act to a large degree on the basis of choice and self-interest, and therefore it seems that influencing the choices which others make, as well as what they perceive to be their self-interest, is a major means of effecting control over what they do. Big men, in fact, are said to lead by force of persuasion and force of personality, which implies that they persuade other people by impressing them in one way or another.

The manipulation of what others believe to be their self-interest emerges, *faute de mieux*, as a major means of influencing their behavior (69). This may take place not only on a one-to-one basis, but on a larger scale as well, between subgroups of the society. One subgroup may influence another by convincing them of a set of beliefs, or ideology, which motivates their behavior. Whether the act of convincing is a conscious one or not is very difficult to address, and I am not arguing that ideological manipulation is necessarily knowingly devious, or done with malice aforethought.

The control by older men over younger men appears to be facilitated by the ideology concerning women, for reasons we have seen, and for others to be taken up in detail later in the chapter. But if we accept that in Highland societies control over others is effected in a major way by manipulation of belief, we might still want to ask why the particular ideology employed in this case should be one concerning women.

As we have seen, older and younger men compete, or potentially compete, for women not simply as sexual partners. Political power for men is crucially dependent upon their success in ceremonial exchange, and this success is in turn critically dependent upon the labor of women. Consequently, control over women and over the access of younger men to women has very important political, as well as economic, ramifications.

The ideology concerning women also happens to reinforce in an important way the two major structural elements which maintain a sense of corporate identity for the local group of men, namely, patrilineality and the men's house. It seems likely that the ideology concerning women may have come into existence originally in conjunction with the maintenance of these crucial institutions, and only secondarily have been adopted, perhaps unconsciously, as a means of control over younger men.

The occasional occurrence of abductions and elopements (70) involving younger men, in conjunction with the prevalent individualism, the lack of structural constraints, and the inapplicability of *force majeur* as coercion, indicate that older men must actually struggle to retain their control over younger men vis à vis women, and that a set of beliefs which renders the women themselves unattractive would be a useful deterrent to the arrogation of women by younger men.

Highland social structure lacks a mechanism, other than the devaluation of women, which would cause younger men to wait with a degree of patience until they become older, with the privileges of older men. For example, there is no formal accession or structural promotion to adulthood and its prerogatives at a specific time in the life cycle, which would provide a definite and foreseeable termination to the relative deprivation of younger men (71). Rather, adult status must be achieved by individual efforts, and yet there are no specific actions which younger men may undertake which will guarantee successful adult status in the future. Some older men do not in fact succeed, and their status as "rubbish men" probably serves as a reminder to younger men that passivity will not be rewarded.

For these reasons, ideology concerning the danger of association with women is a useful and relatively powerful means of constraining the behavior of younger men.

III

There is another major reason that older men inculcate fear and revulsion toward women in younger men. These attitudes contribute to the control by older men over younger men for economic and political purposes, through the manipulation of their marriages and bridewealth payments.

The control through ideology about women is part of a generalized control by older men over adolescents and young people. Langness, for example, notes that "A youth, or a young man, when involved in an argument with an older man on any topic, no matter how right he may be, objectively viewed, will invariably be neutralized, even emasculated, one might say, with something resembling the following: 'You are not a man. You don't have pigs and gardens. You don't have a name. When you do, then you can talk; until then, be quiet.'" (72). Meggitt states that " ... the youth usually remains under his father's jurisdiction ... until he marries [at age 24 or 25]. He has no real control over such socially significant commodities as land, houses, and pigs or over the produce of the family gardens" (73), and that "the bachelor's association provides alternative satisfactions for men who are politically impotent and economically beholden to their married elders" (74). Among the Duna of the Southern Highlands, even men 25-30 years old may be referred to as "nothing boys" by older men (75).

Young men are very often in a difficult structural position; that is, the difficulties of their life situation and of their social situation are engendered by constraints present in the structure of the society of which they are a part. They are expected to procreate eventually, yet they are encouraged to fear women. Their help in cooperative ventures among men, such as fence-building and preparation for fighting (76), is ultimately demanded, yet they are denied a part in the process of distribution and in the allocation of prestige which distribution brings. They are accused of being lazy and irresponsible, yet they do not have scope or reward for responsible behavior of benefit to the community. A young married man is heavily in debt to those who have contributed to his brideprice, yet he has little with which to pay.

Several authors have suggested that hysterical psychotic outbreaks, unique to younger men in most Highland societies, are due to the stresses of a young man's relationships with his affines, his wife, and the older men of his natal group (77). In these transitory occurrences of extreme behavior, a man usually becomes very violent and engages in otherwise forbidden behavior, such as attacking members of his own group, stealing from them, or demanding goods unceremoniously. He shows exaggerated motor activity, brandishing weapons and running through gardens or jogging up and down in one spot, and he seems to be deaf and oblivious to his surroundings, except in some cases to stimuli which directly bear on his demands.

Usually, other residents of the locality attempt to restrain him in a sympathetic manner, although he may provoke laughter or fear as well. There seems to be a recognition of the problems in his life situation, and after the attack of illness, other members of the society may reduce their expectations of him, for example, regarding his future role in exchange. He is not ostracized or stigmatized for his unusual behavior, however.

The arrangement of marriages and bridewealth accumulation for younger men is a source of gain to older men in a number of respects. Young men are allowed very little choice in their own marriages (78). This suggests that the gain which results from their marriages is of considerable importance. It seems likely that control over other people in such a situation is facilitated greatly if the people themselves do not have strong positive preferences or sentiments of their own regarding whom to marry or regarding sex and marriage per se. That is, younger men may be more malleable as avoiders of women than they would be as active pursuers of women. The usually diffident reaction of young men to their marriages, probably due to the anxiety with which they have learned to regard women, does not suggest that they are interested either in actively selecting or in rejecting a mate.

The transfer of wealth as bridewealth payments and as subsequent small return prestations is one of the major forms of exchange in Highland societies, and it is a very important opportunity for a contributor to gain prestige. No young man can raise a brideprice by himself (79), however, apparently because the amount is too great.

This elevated price for women is itself in need of examination. Since the value of women's labor is very great, a "seller's market" could be expected to result. However, the transfer of wealth as bridewealth seems to represent an unusual form of exchange in that the buyers, as well as the sellers, are benefited by a high price.

The prospective groom is far from being the principal buyer, since he has little say in the matter and contributes little to the purchase price. However, the principal buyers, older men who have contributed to his payments, gain an important measure of prestige and political control from their contributions. Since indebting others to oneself appears to be one of the major forms of social control in the Highlands, the older men, as buyers, may be assumed to have reason to keep the brideprice high. It is too high to allow independent action on the part of young men.

On the other hand, an older man, already married, who seeks another wife has a source of wealth through the production of his present wife. He does not depend on other men, and he finds it much easier to amass valuables for the marriage payment on his own (80).

Full adult status is defined, presumably by those who already have it, as being dependent upon marriage (81) and upon participation in economic exchange (82). A young man must marry and subsequently must repay his creditors, in order to achieve a measure of social and political independence. The repayment of creditors, however, is expected at a time when he has few assets and when he cannot yet control the production of his wife (83), and he finds himself in a difficult position.

Those men who never marry, on the other hand, eventually have no independent source of production, and generally become attached to the households of important men in a subservient capacity (84), with the lowest social status (85).

Apart from the gain in political support and prestige to the contributors to a brideprice, the marriage of two young people affects a number of other important economic and political relationships as well. Marriage, which is exogamous, may begin a new trade alliance between groups (86); members of the bride's and groom's groups other than their own families may subsequently be drawn into trade relations by the marriage (87). A major trade relationship may develop between the husband and the wife's brother, and may become independent of the relationship of either to the woman who links them (88).

Bridewealth payments for a daughter are a major source of valuables to an ordinary man. Probably because bridewealth must be returned if a marriage breaks up in its early stages (89), unhappy brides who run away are sent back by their families of origin (90). The situation may have been exacerbated by the dispersal of the bridewealth by the bride's family prior to her running away (91).

Marriages may also begin a new political alliance between two groups (92), or they may be contracted for the purpose of peacekeeping, for example at the cessation of hostilities between two groups (93).

A young bride and groom thus find themselves enmeshed in a complex social situation in which their own wishes are of minimal importance to others. The instability of marriages in their early stages is a commonplace in the Highlands literature (94), and it provides an obvious indicator that the marriages contracted are not to the liking of the people most directly involved.

A. Strathern has suggested that "antagonism between husband and wife is ... likely to be dependent on the degree to which the prospective partners to a marriage are able to choose each other, as well as to the nature of the affinal tie" (95). Sexual avoidance is frequently enjoined upon bride and groom or upon betrothed adolescents (96). The proscription may represent an attempt of the elders' to keep a fragile marriage from dissolving while further bridewealth payments and counter-prestations are still being made.

IV

I argued in the preceding section that the control over male adolescents and young men, by ideology regarding the danger of association with women, is part of a larger social control over younger men (and women) by older men. There are several further respects in which the younger generation is controlled by the older in the Highlands, as well.

The very existence of the category of adolescence in the Highlands may be a further indicator of the social control exercised in the Highlands by one group over another. The conceptual category of adolescence comes from our own society (in which the existence of "adolescence" may also be in need of explanation) and should not for that reason be taken as a given in the argument. That is, adolescence may have a social definition which is dependent upon other factors in the social structure, in the Highlands as well as in our own society.

Socially defined male adolescence in the Highlands appears to begin with the approximate onset of sexual maturity and the strength and ability to do the productive work of an adult, and to end with marriage and participation in economic exchange. Full adult status is dependent upon the successful exchange of goods.

Koch notes in the West Irian Highlands that "By the age of 15 or 16 ... a boy has acquired all necessary skills for independent work in the economic field" (97); since these skills are similar among Highland groups, we can assume that adolescents in other Highland societies are capable of them as well. However, they do not put these skills and physical abilities to use for a number of years. First marriage appears to occur in the early twenties in the group on which Koch reports (98); in other Highland societies the age at first marriage for men is in the mid- to late twenties (99).

The lack of productive labor for male adolescents and young men in the Highlands has been noted by several authors (100). One author (101) describes "[male] children, youths, and young men" as "liv[ing] lives of undisciplined liberty, full of excitement, and free from obligation. Boys and young men do virtually no work and have no chores allotted to them as girls do. A young boy runs and plays with his age mates, chasing birds and rats and whatever he can find, bullying girls - which is actively encouraged by adults - and wandering at his leisure."

Since adolescents possess the necessary skills for productive labor and may be physically stronger and more energetic than adults, the fact that they are granted a special status in which they do not have the responsibilities of adults must be of some significance. The unproductive state of adolescents denies them access to economic power and therefore to political power, keeping them out of the political "arena" in which competition occurs. They cannot even qualify as contenders for the things which adults consider valuable, much less contend sucessfully.

J. Whiting has suggested that violent adolescent rebellion must be prevented "at a time when physical maturity would make such a revolt dangerous and socially disruptive" (102). The prolongation of the irresponsible aspects of childhood may facilitate the prevention of violent rebellion. Similarly, the prolongation in terms of social status of the asexuality of childhood for younger men may facilitate the marriage of older men to young women of the youths' own generation. The younger men may be made more patient, in their wait for the next half-generation of girls to become old enough to marry, by feeling that they are not truly adults, sexually or socially, with rights to young women of their own age.

Lack of productive work and freedom of activity are common among adolescent girls in Highland societies also (103). At first sight this is even more puzzling, given the contribution of adult women and even of female children (104) to production. A little girl works with her mother in the gardens, and may, even as a young child, carry heavy and unwieldy loads of sweet potatoes and thatching grass.

Around the time of puberty, however, and in some cases following a puberty ceremony (e.g., among the Chimbu, the Siane, and the Bena), an adolescent girl ceases almost entirely to work and associates only with other adolescent girls, paying great attention to her appearance. In a number of societies, she no longer sleeps in her mother's house, but in the company of other young people, and spends her time visiting young men in nearby groups during the day and at courting parties during the night.

Here she may have sexual relationships with partners of her own choosing, and at her own initiative, for the only time in her life. It is not surprising that adult women are described as looking back at adolescence nostalgically (105) or with "deep emotion" (106).

It is possible that adolescent girls are allowed considerable freedom from work so that they will be less rebellious vis à vis their impending marriages. They are often not eager to marry in any case (107); were they to have actual experience of the magnitude of their future role in production, they might be still less so.

Another part of the ongoing process of control over younger people may be represented by initiation rites. Nearly all of the Highland societies under discussion have some form of male initiation in the pre-pubertal period, or

Woman with Young Girl and Boys

Young Boys

later in adolescence. These rituals call for forcible separation of the boy from his mother, and may, especially in the Eastern Highlands, involve swallowing long pieces of cane, induced vomiting, bleeding the nose or penis by forcible insertion into the nostrils or urethra of rough leaves rolled into a thin tube, or other forms of incision of the penis.

Letting blood is sometimes equated with menstruation, or it may be intended to release the contaminating influence of the initiates' association with women, that is, primarily with their mothers. I suggest that this harsh treatment (abruptly interrupting the indulgences of childhood) which in the mind of the male child or young adolescent boy might seem to have been caused retrospectively by his mother, predisposes the boy in a dramatic way to fear, distrust, and dislike women, and perhaps to feel that future brutality toward them has been justified by his own suffering. Ritual genital mutilation occuring just prior to marriage, as among the Awa (108), probably predisposes young men to powerful and long-lasting negative associations with women and with sexual relations.

I suggest also that the mother is made to feel helpless about her authority and responsibility for her son, in the face of society's pressure to mark him as its own. He is removed from her sphere of influence by a sudden and harsh mutilation of his body, which she has created and nurtured for many years, and this physical and emotional trauma which occurs to her son must be a demoralizing loss for the mother. Not only is the boy's attachment to his mother weakened, but the mother's feeling of efficacy in protecting her child is undermined. Women in many Highland societies greet the older men returning from initiation ceremonies with weapons, in a form of ritualized attack. It is ritualized because it is destined to be ineffectual in any case, given the role of women in Highland society, but this does not mean that their sentiments are any the less strong.

In some cases, in both the Eastern and Western Highlands, the initiates are also introduced to the cult of the sacred flutes, and there may be a period of seclusion, especially from women. In some societies, such as the Enga and Huli, there are also rituals for older bachelors, which may include irritating the eyes and reiteration of the ideology concerning the dangers of association with women, as well as the benefits of avoiding women.

The data on Highland societies are consistent with J. Whiting's (109) argument that initiation rites for young men are intended to resolve the conflict between the original identification of the young boy with his mother as a love object or as the controller of resources, and the subsequent necessity to transfer his identification to the men of his local group (110). Recent studies have supported this point of view (111), and have demonstrated that gender differentiation is dramatized and reinforced by initiation rites.

I suggest that initiation rites for adolescents and young men may be a part of the general process of control through ideology by older men over the sexuality of younger men, as well. The idea that older men possess secret and life-supporting knowledge to be conveyed under special circumstances may reinforce the willingness of younger men to conform to the expectations of their elders (112). Among the Mae Enga, for example, only older married men possess the magical spells which protect them from the dangers of sexual intercourse; newly married men may buy this information from them (113). Without it, male adolescents and bachelors are effectively deterred by fear from engaging in sexual relations (114). A bachelor who does transgress even once "may irrevocably damage his well-being unless he can induce a married man to sell him at a high price the appropriate protective magic" (115). A similar situation is reported among the Huli (116).

Constraining younger men by fostering in them a feeling of fear and repulsion toward women seems to be a useful and effective means, for older men, of reducing competition for women, and of exercising control over contracted marriages for economic and political gain.

Notes - Chapter Two

1. "But how does it happen that an act whose aim is so solemn, and to which nature invites us with the most powerful of attractions ... has become the most fruitful source of our depravity and our ills?
... It is through the tyranny of man, who has converted the possession of a woman into ownership.

Through customs and habits, which have overloaded the conjugal union with conditions."
2. Read 1954b:867.
3. Langness 1967b:165.
4. Interestingly, many of the symptoms of dissolution with which young men are threatened as a result of association with women mimic the actual aging process. These symptoms include wrinkling and loss of resiliency of the skin, as well as hair loss. Diminished vitality, another threatened occurrence, is matched in actuality by the rapid decrease in respiratory function in Highlands men after the late twenties (Sinnett and Whyte 1973:270).
5. Read 1954b:869; Ryan 1969:167; Salisbury 1969:62; and cf. Gell 1971:169.
6. Read 1954b:870; Berndt 1962:157; Meggitt 1965a:12; Allen 1967:47; Watson 1967b:79; Glasse 1974:82, 84; Buchbinder and Rappaport 1976:21; Newman and Boyd 1982:282; Meigs 1984:21,66.
7. Asad (1979) suggests, in other terms, that it is mistaken to give ideology an "essential and determinate function" as a "basic organizing principle of social life" (ibid:612), without reference to "systematic social connections between historical forces and relations on the one hand, and characteristic forms of discourse sustained or undermined by them on the other" (ibid.:616).
8. Read 1954b:867,870; Berndt 1962:103,111,157; 1965:93; Meggitt 1964:207,221; Newman 1964a:265; Salisbury 1965:162; Langness 1967b:165; A. Strathern 1970a:582; Glasse 1974:82; Newman and Boyd 1982:266; Hays and Hays 1982:214.
9. Newman ibid.
10. Salisbury 1965:65.
11. ibid.
12. Berndt 1962:188; Glasse 1974:82; Buchbinder and Rappaport 1976:21.
13. Read 1954b:869; Reay 1959a:162; Berndt 1962:127; Meggitt 1965a:29; Langness 1967b:171; Bowers 1971:29.
14. Read 1954b:867; Langness 1967b:166; Meggitt 1976:70.
15. Read 1954b:866; Bowers 1965:35; Langness 1965:267; A. Strathern 1972:225. Feil (1986:632) suggests that men's labor in the exchange of pigs should also be considered part of the production process, because pigs "have no social value" (ibid.) without exchange. The meaning of "social value," the social universe in which it applies, and its relationship to the more concrete aspects of production and distribution, are certainly subjects for further scrutiny, but I note here that the benefits of the "social value" of pig exchange accrue mostly to men, and not to the society as a whole.
16. Salisbury 1962:108-109; cf. Godelier and Garanger 1973:217; A. Strathern 1979:6.
17. e.g., Salisbury 1962:49.

18. Read 1954b:866; Berndt 1962:54; Langness 1967b:172; M. Strathern 1972:289.
19. Langness 1967b:172.
20. M. Strathern 1972:99.
21. Lindenbaum 1976:59.
22. Langness 1964:169.
23. Cook 1969:102. Pospisil notes, with regard to the Kapauku of the West Irian Highlands, that "Because a woman has had to be paid for in the form of a bride price, she is regarded by the Kapauku as a financial investment. Consequently, the economically minded Kapauku feels that his investment must be fully exploited by providing the woman with enough work" (Pospisil 1963a:10).
24. Berthoud 1974:307-322; Bohannan and Bohannan 1968: Chapter 16; Dalton 1967:254-256; 260-264; 1971:14-16; Douglas 1967a; 1967b:121-122; DuBois 1936:50-52; Firth 1967:17-21; Frankenburg 1967:71-74; Godelier 1971:65-71; Malinowski 1967:175; Polanyi 1968:138-140; Rosman and Rubel 1971: Chapter 8; Sahlins 1972:213-215; Salisbury 1962: Chapter 8.
25. Rappaport 1968:106.
26. ibid:107.
27. The work load for women appears to be greater in societies with higher levels of pig production (Modjeska 1982:72) and more intensive forms of sweet potato cultivation (ibid:73-74).
28. cf. J.W.M. Whiting and B.B. Whiting 1975:19.
29. Watson 1967b:71.
30. Glasse 1968:48.
31. Bulmer 1971:154.
32. Brookfield and Brown 1963:74; Langness 1967b:162.
33. M. Strathern 1972:44.
34. Reay 1959a:80; ibid:167.
35. Bowers 1965:30.
36. Bowers ibid.; Glasse 1969:26.
37. Bowers 1965; Glasse 1969:26; Waddell 1972:26; and cf. Oosterwal 1959.
38. C. Berndt 1966:254,259; Langness 1969:46; A. Strathern and M. Strathern 1969:145.
39. Ross 1965:427.
40. Hipsley and Kirk 1965:84; Newman 1965:14. Wood and Smouse (1982:410-411) suggest that among the Gainj, there may be a preferential consumption of scarce food by males and females ages 10-30 (who have markedly greater proportional body fat than other age groups).
41. Hipsley and Kirk ibid:8; cf. Johnson 1981:330.
42. 1953, originally 1899:106-107.
43. Read 1952:12; Newman 1964b:9; 1965:79; Langness 1965:266; Lowman-Vayda 1968:213: Glasse 1974:81.
44. Read 1952:14; Meggitt 1964:204,207; Newman 1964a:266.

45. Kelly 1976. Because of the prevalence of overt homosexuality (lacking in the strictly defined Highlands) among the Etoro, it appears to be competition *for* younger men, among older men, younger men, and women, from which the latter two are removed by ideological fright. Kelly's assertion that the "metaphoric relation between two domains of belief [regarding sexual relations and witchcraft]" is "a mechanism for the production of an elementary system of inequality based on age and sex" (ibid:51), is quite relevant to the case of the Highlands, however.

46. Andrew Strathern (1979a) suggests that in the post-colonial cash-crop economy, big men use ideology - in the form of reference to shared values which he does not detail - to persuade women to donate the cash proceeds from coffee-growing to ceremonial exchange, in which women themselves gain no prestige or power. Josephides (1983:306) suggests (with respect to the distinction between pigs raised by women, in which Kewa women have some right of alienation, and pigs acquired by men in exchange, in which women do not have a right of alienation) that successive multiple transactions by men involving pigs acquired by exchange "create a smokescreen in which a woman's labor in the acquisition of exchange pigs is irretrievably lost." She argues that the subsequent exchanges themselves obscure the labor of women in producing the original stock of pigs which allowed exchange to take place (1985:204,208,210).

47. M. Strathern 1972:162.

48. ibid.

49. ibid.

50. ibid:163.

51. ibid:278.

52. M. Strathern (1981:181-2,186) also suggests that personal autonomy of motivation is ascribed to women, in order to "engage their commitment as well as their labor" (ibid:186) to men's endeavors.

53. M. Strathern 1972: Chapter 6. Interestingly, Sexton (1984:140,143) suggests that in the recent past, men in some Eastern Highlands groups have been more willing to acknowledge women's rights in pigs, as money has replaced pigs as the most important prestige item in exchange.

54. Buchbinder and Rappaport 1976:19; LiPuma 1978:40,46.

55. Among the Fore, for example, women eat much less pork than men, and supplement their diets, as men do not, by insects, rodents, frogs, and formerly, human flesh (Lindenbaum 1979:133). Differential (lesser) consumption of pork by women has been noted by other authors as well (LiPuma 1978:47; Gillison 1980:152).

56. There is some variation in Highland groups in this respect, however. Among the Tombema Enga, women can allocate the pigs which they themselves have produced, when the pigs are used for exchange (Feil 1978:270-275).

57. Read 1954a:23; Reay 1959a:192; Berndt 1962:Chapter 9; 1965:358; M. Strathern 1972:282-283; Meggitt 1974:187. Women among the Kewa (Josephides 1985:129) cognizantly acknowledge that they are controlled by men's violence against them.

58. Read 1954a:23; R. Berndt 1962:331,333; Meggitt 1965a:143; Glasse 1968:72; Ryan 1969:173; Bulmer 1971:143; M. Strathern 1972:187; Lindenbaum 1976:59; Modjeska 1982:67.

59. Exact figures for suicide among New Guinea Highlands women are not given, and would probably be rather difficult to ascertain in the field, but it is commented on by a considerable number of authors (v. Table 1.1, Chapter 1). Suicide among women of the Gainj, a people living on the fringe of the Highlands and with many cultural ties to the Highlanders, accounted for 57% of deaths for women 20-49, in a two year period (Johnson 1981:326).

60. Reay 1959a:193; Berndt 1962:409,416.

61. Berndt ibid:398; Reay ibid:192; Sillitoe 1979:83,276.

62. Lawrence and Meggitt 1965:9. Meigs (1984:135) also notes that the Hua belief system lacks "spirits, deities, and the supernatural."

63. Lawrence and Meggitt 1965:14.

64. Reay 1959a:194.

65. ibid.

66. By "unschematized," I mean that the metaphor of pigs (and similarly, of ghosts) is not part of an organized system of categories and oppositions concerning society, nor part of a cosmology which assigns relationships among animals, humans, and other aspects of the natural world. (Cf. M. Strathern 1980, 1984, in which she demonstrates that among the Melpa, wild/domestic, nature/culture, and female/male do not form a consistent set of oppositions.) Although Strathern argues that among the Melpa (who also characterize anti-social behavior as "acting like a wild pig" (1980:198,204)), there is "no particular idea that anti-social propensities lie beneath the surface of every socialized human being" (ibid:198), I would argue that the use of the metaphor, as well as the direct comparison of people to pigs, strongly suggests that people feel "piggish" behavior to be a part, or potential part, of their repertoire, and hence of their "human nature." Even if the comparison is not part of a coherent set of equations between nature and culture, and the people themselves view the natural world and their relationship to it differently than we do, it seems likely that the psychological defense mechanism of projection lies behind these statements - that is, unacceptable characteristics of the individual are split off and attributed to other beings. Of course, an extended discussion of the logical and psychological aspects of metaphor belongs, and can be found, elsewhere.

Gillison, on the other hand, does present the beliefs of the Gimi of the Eastern Highlands, concerning male and female, the wild and the mundane, continuity of existence and death, and other oppositions (1980:153,161), as part of an internally consistent cosmology. The problem here, in brief, is that she does not sufficiently distinguish among (a) the beliefs of the Gimi, as they themselves would state them, (b) her own interpretation of their beliefs, and (c) extrapolation from what she takes to be their unconscious beliefs. Gillison herself says that "what we might call conscious, preconscious, and unconscious associations are run together" (ibid:152). Without stating it as such, she has used a somewhat narrowly construed classical Freudian model to interpret symbols in the unconscious, and it would be possible to argue that it is she who has made their thoughts and feelings into a "cosmological system." Here again the philosophical underpinnings of these problems warrant discussion in some other context.

67. Reay: 1959a:192.
68. Newman 1965:92.
69. Even patrilineality, the major ideological commitment which infuses socially oriented behavior, is a construct (not corresponding with the reality of recruitment) which may be used in an ambiguous fashion for the pursuit of individual aims (see discussion, Chapter Three).
70. Read 1954b: 868; Koch 1968a:96; Cook 1969:102; Langness 1969:45; Rappaport 1969:129.
71. cf. Maybury-Lewis 1967:159.
72. Langness 1965:269.
73. Meggitt 1965a:247.
74. Meggitt 1964:217.
75. Modjeska 1982:63. A. Strathern (1982:47) points out that inequalities between seniors and juniors in the Mt. Hagen area are not part of a "class" system, as has been suggested for West Africa, since Melpa fathers encourage the entry of the their sons into moka (competitive, prestige-oriented exchange), and fathers do not retain productive forms of property until their death. Modjeska (1982:59-63) discusses other dissimilarities with the West African case, including the lack in the Highlands of expropriation of the surplus value of juniors' labor, the lack of appropriation and redistribution of vegetable staple food by elders, and minimal requirements for technical knowledge and for coordination of labor on the part of elders in the Highlands - all of which diminish the extent of their authority as compared with the West African case. The sexual division of labor is also much more pronounced in the New Guinea Highlands.
76. Langness 1965:268.
77. Read 1954b:870; Newman 1964b:9; Langness 1965:266.
78. Langness 1965:266; 1967b:169; Meggitt 1965b:111; Koch 1968a:96; Glasse 1969:22; Rappaport 1969:128; Ryan 1969:95. In the period since the mid-1970's, however, this situation has changed considerably in some localities.

79. Newman 1964b:10; Bowers 1965:33; Langness 1967b:167; 1969:40; Brown 1969:84; Meggitt 1969:6; Rappaport 1969:131.
80. Newman 1964b:12; Ryan 1969:175.
81. Read 1954a:28; 1954b:867; Meggitt 1965b:114; Langness 1969:40.
82. Newman 1964b:9; Langness 1965:265.
83. Newman 1964b:10-11.
84. Vicedom and Tischner 1943, Vol 2:48; Gitlow 1948:36; Bowers 1965:36; Meggitt 1965a:43; Brown 1972:41; Waddell 1972:102, 189-190.
85. A. Strathern (1982:46-47) notes that status differences between big men and ordinary men are not part of a "class system" because, among other reasons, inequalities of status are not reproduced from one generation to another.
86. Barnes 1962:8; M. Strathern 1972:66.
87. Meggitt 1965a:157; Koch 1968a:105; Brown 1969:79, 81; M. Strathern 1972:65,77-78.
88. Reay 1959a:62-64; Brown 1964:348; Langness 1969:53; M. Strathern 1972:222.
89. Langness 1969:49; Ryan 1969:174; M. Strathern 1972:190.
90. Koch 1968a:104; Brown 1969:90; Cook 1969:103; Langness 1969:45; Ryan 1969:167.
91. Reay 1959a:76; Rappaport 1969:140; Ryan 1969:167.
92. Ryan 1969:175.
93. Brown 1964:351; Rappaport 1969:128; M. Strathern 1972:70,199; Hayano 1974:288-289.
94. Read 1954a:28; Brown 1964:343; 1969:84; 93; Newman 1964b:11; Langness 1967b:169; Cook 1969:106; Rappaport 1969:130; Ryan 1969:167; M. Strathern 1972:99,195; Glasse 1974:84.
95. A. Strathern 1969a:43.
96. Read 1954b:867; Newman 1964b:9; Bowers 1965:33; Langness 1965:266; Meggitt 1965b:127; Salisbury 1965:62; Meigs 1984:105.
97. Koch 1968a:90.
98. ibid:96.
99. Meggitt 1965a:86; Glasse 1969:26; Waddell 1972:24.
100. Langness 1965:266; 1967b:166; Brown 1972:52; Waddell 1972:103.
101. Langness: ibid.
102. J. Whiting et al 1958:361.
103. Reay 1959a:176; Langness 1965:267; 1969:42; Newman 1965:97; Ross 1965:423; Salisbury 1965:73; Brown 1969:83; Waddell 1972:103.
104. Reay ibid; Salisbury ibid; Langness 1967b:167.
105. Reay ibid:175.
106. Ross:ibid.
107. Reay 1959a:179; Brown 1964:344; Langness 1967b:169.

108. Newman and Boyd 1982.
109. J. Whiting et al 1958; Burton and Whiting 1961.
110. Some of the discussion of male initiation rites in the Highlands (Allen 1967; A. Strathern 1970b; Koch 1974) has involved problems of definition and methodology whose complexities are not entirely relevant here.
111. Herdt 1982; Newman and Boyd 1982; Hays and Hays 1982.
112. Keesing notes that "access to cultural meaning is a crucial aspect of the political structure" (1982:38).
113. Meggitt 1964:210.
114. Meggitt 1965a:104.
115. ibid.
116. Glasse 1968:52.

"Il sait calculer tout ce qu'un homme peut se permettre d'horreurs sans se compromettre; et pour etre cruel et méchant sans danger, il a choisi les femmes pour victimes" (1).
P.A. Choderlos de la Clos, *Les Liaisons Dangereuses*, 1782

3

The Social Matrix of the Relationship Between the Sexes

I

In searching for an explanation of antagonism on the part of men toward women in the New Guinea Highlands, we need to look beyond the relationship between men and women per se to the larger structure of social relationships in which the relationship between the sexes is enmeshed.

The structure of relations among men themselves seems to be the set of relationships with the most crucial bearing upon antagonism between the sexes.

But before developing this argument, we might ask why we should not give equal attention to the relationship of women with one another, if only for the sake of parity. There are several reasons, however, that the structural relationships of women to one another do not determine the relationships among men or between men and women in the same way as the relationships among men determine those among women and between the sexes.

Because of virilocality, a woman always marries into a local group of men with some conception of itself as a corporate group, and leaves her family of origin, which is itself a local group of men with corporate ideology and in-marrying women. The predominant patrilineal ideology reinforces the notion of the male corporate group. Even the manner in which children are thought to be made, in some Highland groups, reinforces the notion that the important substance of life comes from the father, with the mother as a kind of passive growing-medium (2).

The denial of most jural rights to women (3) means that they are less able to control their own fates than are men, and that they certainly have less influence over community decision making. Men are in complete control of political decisions, including those which affect women.

Women do not form a corporate work group; their work is generally done alone and involves little cooperative effort (4). The suggestion by Robert Murphy (5), that antagonism between the sexes is fundamental to differentiation necessary for the maintenance of corporate work groups, would therefore not be applicable to the New Guinea Highlands situation.

Women do not seem to have an ideology of themselves as a corporate group (6), although they do not entirely accept the marginal role in society assigned to them by men, either. The opinions of women as to their roles and statuses are under-reported in the literature. The work of Marilyn Strathern (7) is a notable exception. According to information she presents, women do to some degree see themselves as members of their own natal groups, particularly with respect to their relationships with their brothers. In general, women maintain ties of affection with their brothers and encourage their husbands to pursue an active alliance with them, often urging their husbands to trade with their brothers in preference to other trading partners. Reay also states that "The values [a girl] ... has learned are those of an agnatic descent group ... It is always with a group of men that a woman identifies herself" (8).

Consequently, in-marrying adult women probably never feel themselves to be unambivalent members of one social group. The problem is further exacerbated by the fact that the group from which an in-marrying wife originates may be inimical to the husband's group, either generally hostile (9) or intermittently hostile (10). Women may therefore have conflicting loyalties to two inimical societies.

Meggitt, in one of the early articles written on sexual antagonism in the Highlands, suggested that marriage between people from groups inimical to one another was positively correlated with fear of pollution and a low status of women (11). This suggestion has subsequently been disputed on several grounds, including the difficulties involved in defining and measuring the status of women in the Highlands (12), the importance of factors other than warfare, such as affinal ceremonial exchange, in determining relations between affines (13), and the fact that fear of pollution occurs in societies "where marriage is not predominately with enemies, for example in Hagen [Melpa] and Chimbu" (14). Brown (15) has also noted that the married pair and both sets of affines may maintain friendly relations among themselves, despite the enmity of their respective groups, and Feil (16) states that exchange between affines belonging to enemy groups may help to mitigate or end hostilities between the groups.

A further reason for the non-alignment of women into a corporate group or counter-group of their own is that there may be other women married into the husband's group who come from groups traditionally inimical to a woman's own natal group. Some of the in-marrying women may have been her sexual rivals in the past (17). The loyalty of a woman to her husband's group in opposition to an inimical group may also be lessened by the fact that she may know the men of the inimical group as former suitors (18), or as former allies of her own natal group.

Incorporation into the husbands' group is not only a matter of the women's sentiments concerning their own loyalty, however. They are also thought to have conflicting loyalties by the men of the group into which they marry, and in some groups are suspected of poisoning or sorcery (19), at the suggestion of their own natal kin. Regardless of their own sentiments, their lack of full incorporation into the husbands' group has much to do with the outright refusal by men to grant them this status, through the denial to women of political power and participation in ritual activity.

Finally, women may be in a situation of competition rather than cooperation with one another, because a woman may be in competition for several scarce resources with her husband's other wives or with his mother or unmarried sisters (20). These scarce resources may include the husband's aid with garden work, allocation by the husband of garden land (21), or trade by the husband with her cognates. The pigs and other goods produced by a woman may be disposed of in trade by her husband for a purpose against her wishes. For example, a wife may wish her husband to use the pigs she has raised to trade with her brother or to make payments for children or delayed payments for herself, while the husband may use these pigs to acquire another wife or to trade with another wife's affines. Struggles over the allocation of goods produced by the wife are a major source of disagreement between husband and wife (22).

In short, women's relationships with one another are very dissimilar to men's relationships with one another, because of their structural position as in-marrying strangers, their lack of corporate identity and corporate function (both in production and politically), their competition with one another, their potentially conflictual friendships and enmities, and their lack of political power vis à vis men. Consequently, the effect of their relationships with one another upon the relationship between the sexes does not have the same strength as does the effect of the parallel set of relationships among men.

II

The effect of relationships among men on the relationship between the sexes, on the other hand, is very powerful. In this chapter and the next, I will argue that several kinds of social structural factors are significant in generating tension between the sexes, among them the "loose structure" of Highland groups, the conflicting loyalties generated by "loose structure," the achievement of local "solidarity" by the manipulation of ideology, and the prestige system and the personality generated by competition for prestige.

There has been a lengthy and continuing debate in the Highlands literature on the extent to which Highland societies can be characterized as patrilineal, or on what other basis local groups are structured (23). This discussion stems from an older debate in British social anthropology about the meaning of lineality and filiation in various contexts.

The problem in the Highlands situation is that although the people themselves characterize their own groups as patrilineal, and a patrilineal ideology is invoked as a charter or in a normative fashion, the actual recruitment to the local group comes from a variety of sources; in addition to the agnatic mode of recruitment, cognatic and affinal modes are employed, and even "friends" and non-relatives may be actively recruited to the local group, or accepted as refugees from elsewhere.

This contradiction, which has sometimes been characterized as "loose structure," has given rise to an extensive discussion about the role of lineality and ideology regarding lineality, and about the ways of describing the social structure of these societies with fluctuating membership. A fine summary of these arguments can be found elsewhere (24).

I would suggest that the discrepancy between the ideology about group composition, and the actual group composition itself, plays a major role in determining social relations. It seems likely that this major structural contradiction has an effect upon the relationship between the sexes as well.

Highland societies are characterized by a shifting composition of personnel (25). It has been suggested that the fluctuating character of Highland societies is due to migration and dispersion caused by warfare (26), to the need to absorb new personnel for the purpose of defense (27), to the attempts of big men to gain more adherents for themselves, either vis à vis local factions or vis à vis big men in other localities (28), to the fact that there is little capital investment held jointly by the lineage or inherited through lineality (29), and to the lack of storable food (30).

Another underlying factor which may possibly contribute to the shifting alignment of population is the stress between the need to limit the number of offspring in a given local area, and the need to increase, in the local area, the number of adult men for the purpose of defense and of adult women for the production of goods for ceremonial exchange.

The fluctuating character of the society's personnel and composition affects many other aspects of Highland social organization, which in turn affect the relationship between the sexes.

The conflicting loyalties and alignments which the fluidity of the social structure generates lead to an over-emphasis on maleness as a principle of inclusion in social groups, and to the projection of dissension onto women, as I will show later in the chapter.

In the subsequent chapter, we will see that the fluidity of the social structure and the lack of formally constituted authority also give rise to competition for prestige and the need to lead by force of personality, and to the development of a range of personality characteristics which enable the individual man to turn social situations to his own advantage. Because men make decisions mostly on the basis of self-interest, influencing what others believe is an important means of social control. In certain ways ideology, especially about women, seems to be used to constrain other people in the absence of formal institutions of authority.

The problem of group definition and structure is not limited to the disparity between the patrilineal ideology and the actual composition of the group, however. A number of other factors may tend to increase friction in the local group and make a clear-cut definition of the corporate group, even at the local level, difficult.

For example, A. Strathern (31) suggests that reasons for affiliation (other than agnation) may include matrifiliation, co-residence, and participation in exchange or cult rituals. Individuals have a great deal of latitude in choosing their affiliations, e.g., for the purpose of residence (32).

Big men especially make use of many ties, and may have ties of their own which are unrelated to the alliances of the group to which they belong (33). Sahlins (34) has suggested that a big man's trade partners in other groups may compete for scarce resources with his followers in the local group.

On the other hand, Newman suggests that members of the local group think of themselves as a group "held together not so much by one kind of genealogical tie as by ties of reciprocity among themselves and allegiance to a 'big man' ... the sources of integration are much more in the power structure than in the kinship structure" (35).

Apart from the manner of recruitment to the local group, there are other kinds of shifting personnel in groups and cross-cutting alliances, as well. For example, as noted previously, the families of a bride and groom may be in an alliance relationship even when the local groups to which each family belongs are outright enemies (36). Meggitt states that "groups at different levels in the same hierarchy [of exogamic prohibitions] may be involved in different or even conflicting patterns of exchange and marriage" (37). According to Langness, "the number and kinds of individual ties that can be formed are almost infinite" (38). For example, the contributors to a bride price and to subsequent prestations to the bride's family do not form a stable group. Rather, they contribute on an ad hoc basis, depending on whether they "have something available at that moment" (39).

Not only alliances, but hostilities as well, may follow a confused pattern (40). For example, Brown describes the following situation, which might almost be called "the war of all against all":

> As the war progressed, however, the alignment of opponents became less clear. Individuals joined in to support each side. These were often nonagnatic kinsmen and affines of the members of the sides, and particularly of the protagonists and leaders. Some were co-residents and dependents of the people they supported. These might bring in other members of their groups who enjoyed the excitement of battle without having a grievance, or who had their own reasons for wanting to injure the enemy. On such an individual basis, members of clans and tribes not concerned in the dispute entered the fight, sometimes on both sides. Other groups also joined the fray ... A group with a standing grievance against one side might take advantage of its enemy's position to attack it, without joining forces with the latter's opponent ... In such situations the allies did not usually form a single army ... In a number of cases the bereaved [allied] group considered its ally responsible and attacked it to avenge its loss. This became a separate, simultaneous fight which did not involve the turncoats in an alliance with their former enemy ... At some stage in a conflict parts of a tribe were often found on opposing sides, each with extra-tribal allies. Sometimes part of a tribe fought with the outside enemy against its own fellow tribesmen" (41).

In view of the confused pattern of alliances and hostilities outlined above, it is not surprising that men of the local group may have conflicting loyalties (42). Multiple affiliation may also be detrimental to local solidarity (43). Langness has suggested that "the foundation of the New Guinea social order would collapse" if men's loyalties to their wives were greater than to their fellows (44). I note that the loyalties of wives, if taken account of by men of the local group, would add to the complexity of the situation by an order of magnitude, in geometric rather than linear progression.

Despite all of the stresses on the integrity of the local group, including its mixed composition, the local group does maintain a patrilineal ideology, asserting that all male members of the group (who are not obviously newcomers) are descended from related male ancestors. This has been reported for all Highland groups (45). At the same time, shallow genealogies seem to be universal for the Highlands area (46). This means that people are unable to remember the pattern of descent (or ascent) for more than two or three generations prior to their own. The corollary of shallow genealogy, that is, the granting of fictional agnation after one to three generations (47), is also universal for the Highlands area. Male co-residents of some duration are thought of as being related through a male ancestor regardless of their true origin.

In the extensive Highlands literature on the meaning of patrilineal kinship in a situation of bilateral and other forms of recruitment, some of the most useful suggestions as to the role of patrilineal "descent dogmas" have been made by Andrew Strathern. He suggests that "agnatic descent constructs ... are not made the basis of rigidly maintained jural rules determining inheritance and succession. Rather they are employed as moral symbols, as assertions of stability and solidarity in a world of flux, drawing men together against the divisive pulls of their extra-patrifilial ties" (48). He further suggests that assertions of descent from "one father" "are in the realm of assertions about identity, continuity, and unity" and "mirror critical delimitations of rights and duties toward clansmen" (49), and that "the descent idiom ... provides a logical model for relations of exclusiveness and inclusiveness between group segments" (50).

At the same time, the Highlanders themselves seem to be conscious that there is a degree of ambiguity in the ascription of agnation, and to make use of this ambiguity on occasion, for the purpose of inclusion and exclusion (51).

Strathern employs the concept of "solidarity" in the statement quoted above, as have numerous others who have written about the Highlands. Reference has been made to "lineage solidarity" (52) and to "group solidarity"(53), and many references have been made to "male solidarity" (54).

The concept of "male solidarity" deserves an extended discussion in another context, especially because the concept may rest on some implicit and unexamined ethnocentric assumptions stemming from our own society. Here, at least, we could ask what some of the functions of "solidarity" might be. Apart from the connotation of semi-mystical bonding which the notion of solidarity might suggest, we could assume that group "solidarity" or cohesion is necessary for the men of a locality to form some kind of corporate identity for themselves, for minimizing dissension within the local group, and for the smooth coordination of activities pertaining to ceremonial exchange and to defense and offense in the endemic warfare of the region.

Maintaining group strength is crucial for defense, and common defense of a local territory seems to be one of the most significant measures by which a group may be defined. Rappaport, for example, states that "Tsembaga are a corporate entity in warfare and in the major rituals ... " (55); A. Strathern notes that " ... local political groups consist of sets of males who hold, or attempt to hold, their territory against other similar groups" (56). According to Langness, "... the commitment to maintain the group strength is as much a part of the ideology as the notion of patrilineal descent" (57); Newman states that "the cohesiveness of this [local] group ... derives primarily from occupying a common territory, acting in common defense, and feeling a continuity with the past" (58).

Despite the widespread use of the concept of male solidarity noted above, there are many respects in which the concept requires further exploration, in particular the articulation of male solidarity with other social institutions, and some of the processes by which male solidarity might be maintained.

I would suggest that the exclusion of women from ritual, the explicit devaluation of women's worth and the concomitant emphasis on the value of being a man, the idea that women are divisive and disruptive, and the view of women as a mysterious and dangerous unknown quantity, may be explained in part by the significant contribution of these attitudes to a feeling of sameness, cohesiveness, and fellowship among men who may in fact have little in common or who may be subject to numerous stresses in their relationships among themselves. Women are the logical contrastive "other"; by seeing women as outsiders, the men of a local group make themselves "insiders" with respect to one another (59).

I would suggest also that the complex of attitudes toward women outlined above serves many of the same functions as the universal granting of fictional agnation, but that it serves as an important mechanism of incorporation *before* fictional agnation can be granted.

Much attention has been given in the literature to the existence of fictional agnation, shallow genealogies, and the discrepancy between the actual group composition and the group's ideology about it. However, the significance of the fact that fictional agnation is not granted until the newcomers have resided among the local group for at least one, and in most cases two or three, generations, does not seem to have been noted previously; rather, the granting of fictional agnation has generally been treated as a process of "rapid assimilation" (60). In fact, the lag of one to three generations is extremely important, for the same stresses which give rise to the granting of fictional agnation and to shallow genealogies are at least as much in operation during the interim as they are after several generations have passed.

It is important to note that many crucial structural realignments can occur within one generation in the Highlands. Groups may be dispersed and parts of the group may take residence elsewhere; big men rise to power and then decline, causing a realignment of their supporters; exchange relationships among groups and among individuals alter; and enmity and alliance among groups may alter. Newcomers may be accepted from elsewhere who bring with them their own sentiments of alliance and enmity.

As the composition of groups and alliances alters, loyalties (61) must change in an important way as well. For example, a group which takes up residence elsewhere may suddenly find itself the enemy of a former ally or vice versa. In a situation of fluctuating loyalties, the necessity for some unchanging mode which generates a feeling of inclusion and identity for men of the local group is particularly great. It is interesting to note in this conjunction that the social definition of sex roles is a constant in the Highlands, as is the division of labor between the sexes. The comparative stability of these structural factors is itself of significance.

Mary Douglas has argued that the body may be used to represent the social structure (62); Buchbinder and Rappaport have noted that using the distinction between male and female for social purposes is not simply a matter of making use of a metaphor about things which can be looked upon objectively apart from the self. Rather, the self becomes part of the metaphor, which therefore becomes "inescapable" (63). It is possible that this inescapability adds to the permanence of the distinction between the sexes.

Stressing the dichotomy between the sexes, and using the dichotomy as a metaphor of inclusion and exclusion, seem to help in an important way to resolve potential conflict among men of the local group. Langness, for example, has emphasized the necessity for "male solidarity" for the purpose of defense in warfare (64); Watson states that the group of former refugees who have "overnight become indispensable" as a part of the local group are "invited to reside with men of the older sibs ... [of the original local group] in one of the men's houses [of the original group]" in order to encourage it to "give up its erstwhile alien status and distinct social ties" (65). A. Strathern notes that the men's house (66) may serve as what might be called an alternative metaphor of incorporation (apart from kinship), as can the "garden division" (67) and the "consumption of food grown on clan land" (68).

As a process, the overemphasis on maleness, in the face of a differing reality, has a parallel in the overemphasis on clanship. According to Reay, "The Kuma's consciousness that the clan is by no means permanent or unchanging is accompanied by an overemphasis of clanship and an insistence on its continuance" (69).

Apart from shifting group composition, factionalism, and the resulting changes of loyalty, there are other significant structural stresses among men of the local group. These may include rivalry between brothers (70), or between father and son (71). "Inferior status" or "second class citizenship" (probably translatable into differences in standard of living and in access to women and power) for newcomers vis à vis older residents of a locality (72), and for bachelors vis à vis married men (73), are another source of structural stress in the society. Tensions arising from intraclan competition for prestige (74), and the conflict between older and younger generations of men (which we have looked at already) are other potential sources of conflict.

The friction which some of these stresses may generate in the local group requires more emphasis than it has previously received, especially because the cohesion necessary for defense may be significantly undermined by these conflicts.

The quality of being male, as opposed to female, is something which all men of the local group obviously have in common. Elevating this distinction to a principle of inclusion and exclusion and endowing it with a mystique may help the men of the locality to disregard or minimize their own conflicting loyalties and statuses.

It appears also that men project dissension among themselves onto women. That is, instead of overtly recognizing that they have differences with one another, they attribute the causes of dissension to women (75). Women are characterized as disloyal and disruptive (76). According to M. Strathern " ... events may be attributed to the woman's disposition, in a context ... of mutual suspicions between the men" (77). She also states that "blaming women is one way in which the men protest their innocence" (78); similarly, "the mutual interests of brothers-in-law is expressed in men's tendency to blame the wife when a marriage does break up" (79). Interestingly, in view of the pronounced structural conflict in Highland society between individual self-interest on the part of men, and the interests of the group as a whole, "unaligned self-interest is portrayed as typically female" (80).

Adultery by men within the local group is condoned in many Highland groups (81), at least by men; the husband may express his anger toward his adulterous wife, but not at the man involved, if he is a member of the local group, although a similar offense would be sufficient cause to start a feud with a neighboring group.

The manner in which children are thought to be produced, namely, that it takes repeated acts of intercourse by the same man to impregnate a woman (82), ensures that a casual affair is not thought to lead to pregnancy, and consequently, that the social father of a child remains the mother's husband. This belief probably serves to minimize friction among men of the local group also.

In addition to the projection of dissension among themselves, it seems very likely that the sensation of being in constant danger, in a situation of endemic warfare and raiding, is projected by men onto women, whose "dangers" are more easily controlled than the real ones. I note in this conjunction that in several groups, beliefs about fertility and sexuality seem to be inextricably linked to beliefs about other anxiety-provoking subjects, such as death and rotting (83).

Thus it seems that in a number of ways, sentiments about women may be generated by factors which have little to do with women themselves.

Notes - Chapter Three

1. "He knows how to calculate all the horrors that a man can permit himself without compromising himself; and to be cruel and wicked without danger, he has chosen women as victims."
2. Read 1954a:24; Reay 1959a:75.
3. M. Strathern 1972: Chap 11; Meggitt 1964:220-221; Watson 1970:111.
4. Koch 1968a:87; M. Strathern 1972:23,27,274; Brown and Buchbinder 1976:4.
5. Murphy 1959:96-97.
6. Nor do women, according to M. Strathern (1978), have a value system alternate to the male-oriented system of prestige which tends to devalue them (ibid:183,184,198).
7. M. Strathern 1972.
8. Reay 1959a:182; cf. Josephides 1985:135.
9. Meggitt 1964:18.
10. M. Strathern 1972:67.
11. Meggitt 1964:219-222. Walter (1978) has attempted to extend this analysis.
12. A. Strathern 1969a:42.
13. ibid:43; Feil 1980:32-33.
14. A. Strathern ibid:43.
15. Brown 1964:335.
16. Feil 1980:27,38.
17. Reay 1959a:183.
18. Reay ibid; M. Strathern 1972:83.
19. Brown 1964:354; Read 1954a:27; M. Strathern 1972:164.

20. Lamphere (1974:105) has suggested that competition among affinally related women is typical of patrilocal, patrilineal societies.
21. Meggitt 1965a:246; Koch 1968a:102-103; M. Strathern 1972:22,27,52,57.
22. Newman 1965:41; Cook 1969:108; M. Strathern 1972: Chap. 6. The central importance of exchange in Highland society has been dealt with at length by Rubel and Rosman (1978).
23. Read 1954a; Barnes 1962; Brown 1962; Langness 1964; Meggitt 1965a; Kaberry 1967; de Lepervanche 1967, 1968; A. Strathern 1969a; 1972; 1973; Watson 1970; Wagner 1974; Mandeville 1978.
24. de Lepervanche 1967; 1968; A. Strathern 1969a.
25. Wagner 1974: Watson 1970.
26. Barnes 1962:9; Brookfield and Brown 1963:79; Koch 1968a:87; Mandeville 1979:112. The magnitude of dispersal due to warfare is indicated by Meggitt (1977:15). Six separate total defeats and evictions in Enga localities resulted in the dispersion of at least 1500 people, and the losing clans or subclans ceased to exist as autonomous units (ibid:114).
27. Langness 1964:173; Kaberry 1967:122.
28. Kaberry 1967:118,121-122; de Lepervanche 1968:177; Watson 1970:115,119; A. Strathern 1972:214,227-228.
29. Barnes 1962:8; Langness 1964:169; A. Strathern 1972:214-215.
30. Barnes 1962:9.
31. A. Strathern 1969a:38.
32. Barnes 1962:6,7; Brown 1962:61; Langness 1964:170; 1969:54; Kaberry 1967:113.
33. Barnes 1962:7; de Lepervanche 1967:149; 1968:177.
34. Sahlins 1968:167.
35. Newman 1965:59. Biersack (1984:123) notes that the solidarity of the local group among the Paiela "is predicated on cooperation in the exchange context."
36. Brown 1964:336; A. Strathern 1969a:49.
37. Meggitt 1969:10.
38. Langness 1969:52.
39. ibid.
40. Read 1954b:865.
41. Brown 1964:351.
42. Barnes 1962:7; Glasse 1969:22; Watson 1970:111.
43. Barnes ibid.
44. Langness 1974:208.
45. e.g., Read 1954a:11; Reay 1959a:33; Brown 1962:67; Langness 1964:164-165; Kaberry 1967:114; A. Strathern 1973:25.
46. e.g., Reay 1959a:34; Barnes 1962:6; Langness 1964:172; Watson 1970:115: A. Strathern 1973:28.

47. e.g., Barnes 1962:6; Brown 1962:115; Meggitt 1965a:32-35; de Lepervanche 1967:153; Watson 1970:113; Lowman-Vayda 1971:332; A. Strathern 1972:219; 1973:27.
48. A. Strathern 1972:215-216.
49. ibid:220.
50. ibid:222.
51. Reay 1959a:34,36; Meggitt 1965a:44; Kaberry 1967:123; A. Strathern 1973:27,32; Feil 1978b:267. Feil (ibid.; 1978a) actually describes the process in reverse: that men among the Tombema Enga convert agnates into non-agnates to facilitate exchange relationships. But this still suggests a play on the ambiguity of ascribed kinship.
52. Reay 1959a:61; Koch 1968b:137.
53. Read 1954a:32; Langness 1964:180-181; de Lepervanche 1968:181; A. Strathern 1969a:42; Koch 1974:414.
54. Read 1952:16; 1954a:25; 1954b:866,868; Reay 1959b:290; de Lepervanche 1967:145; Langness 1967b:162; 1969:53; 1974:199-200; A. Strathern 1969a:44; 1970a:581,583; 1970b:375; 1973:25; Modjeska 1982:108; and cf. Barth 1975:67,245; Herdt 1982:83; Keesing 1982:9,36; Newman and Boyd 1982:241. Read (1982:69) also refers to "the particular phallic sense of masculine identity bonding members of the male community."
55. Rappaport 1969:118.
56. A. Strathern 1972:225.
57. Langness 1964:169.
58. Newman 1965:31.
59. The Huli of the Southern Highlands, who apparently have the greatest degree of cognatic recruitment of all Highland societies (Glasse 1968:30-31) (while still conferring advantages upon agnates (ibid:43-44) and maintaining that they are descended from brothers (ibid:23)), also seem to have the most exaggerated fear of pollution, measured in terms of avoidance by men of women under nearly all circumstances.
60. e.g., Watson 1970:113.
61. Brown 1964:352; de Lepervanche 1967:147; Hayano 1974:289.
62. Douglas 1966b: Chap. 7.
63. Buchbinder and Rappaport 1976:33.
64. Langness 1967b.
65. Watson 1970:117.
66. A. Strathern 1972:231.
67. ibid:222.
68. A. Strathern 1973:28-29.
69. Reay 1959a:36.
70. Read 1954a:16; Reay 1959a:60 et passim; Berndt 1962:81-82; Langness 1965:264; Watson 1970:120; Modjeska 1982:64.
71. Meggitt 1965a:248; 1976:67.

72. Meggitt 1965a:44; de Lepervanche 1967:153, regarding the Mendi, Mae Enga, and Kuma; Ryan 1969:170; Watson 1970:122.

73. Vicedom and Tischner 1943, Vol. 2:48; Reay 1959a:71; Bowers 1965:36; Meggitt 1965a:43; Brown 1969:95; A. Strathern and M. Strathern 1969:150.

74. Feil 1980:20,36.

75. cf. Collier and Rosaldo (1981:296,299) regarding women as "trouble-causing" scapegoats for conflict among "harmonious" men in uxorilocal, brideservice, hunter-gatherer and hunter-horticulturalist societies.

76. M. Strathern 1972:184,186; Buchbinder and Rappaport 1976:31; and cf. Collier 1974:92.

77. M. Strathern 1972:218.

78. ibid:238.

79. ibid:310.

80. M. Strathern 1981:175.

81. Read 1954b:866; Berndt 1962:160; Brown 1969:94; Langness 1969:45; 1974:204.

82. Reay 1959a:75,83; Brown 1969:83; M. Strathern 1972:42,43; Langness 1974:204; Biersack 1984:129.

83. A. Strathern 1970a:581-582; Buchbinder and Rappaport 1976; Gillison 1980:149,153; Meigs 1984:35.

4

Socio-Economic Structure and Personality

I

Men of the New Guinea Highlands have generally been described as shrewd, self-vaunting, individualistic, opportunistic, manipulative, self-aggrandizing, quarrelsome, aggressive, violent, flamboyant, boastful, and hypersensitive to insult (1). These characteristics are descriptive, but they are also normative, because they are considered to be desirable by men of the Highlands themselves.

It seems rather obvious that the expression of personality characteristics of this kind must have some effect on the relationship between men and women. In this chapter I will look at several related questions. Where does this constellation of personality characteristics come from? How may it be tied to other factors in the social or economic structure? Given certain socio-economic or political constraints present in the structure of the society, what useful purpose might these characteristics serve? What is the effect of these characteristics on the relationship between men and women? Conversely, how may the characteristics themselves be an effect of the structural relationship between men and women as well as of other structural relationships?

It is useful to clarify some concepts here. Without entering into a complex philosophical discussion, we might say that "personality characteristics" can be seen as a set of dispositions to behave in certain ways. These dispositions manifest themselves in behavior, and the behavior shows a pattern, with a high frequency of certain similar actions. A patterned frequency may be seen in an individual over time; patterned frequency of behavior may also be seen in an aggregate of individuals, members of the same society or subgroup of a society.

In speaking of a "modal personality," or of personality characteristics which most men of the Highlands share, I am referring mostly to their observable, patterned, socially oriented behavior. I do not have direct reference to the internal psycho-dynamic states of individuals, nor to their subjective emotions, their unconscious drives and conflicts, or their internal symbolic representations of reality. (Some aspects of these things may be implied in a description of behavior, however.)

It has to be said that this is most unfortunate. The phenomena just mentioned, if known, would give valuable insight into the motivation of individuals to act as they do, particularly in regard to an issue as charged with meaning psychologically as the relationship between the sexes.

The Highlanders of New Guinea have not been studied from this perspective (2), however, and it would not be easy to do so. Dreams, free associations, unstructured interviews in which repetitive patterns emerge, life history, and sometimes projective tests are the usual subject matter through which the unconscious conflicts, identifications, defenses, etc. of an individual are studied. These methods are time consuming and require a type of training unfamiliar to most anthropologists, and they are not easily undertaken on a large scale in a field setting (3).

Even if the subjective states, unconscious conflicts, and so forth of some individuals were ascertained, many knotty problems would remain concerning the integration of these data into a theory about society, rather than about individuals. Individuals are motivated by individual forces, and yet it is what they have in common that concerns us in the study of society, not their individual idiosyncracies. The very fact that they have certain characteristics in common suggests that the ultimate causes of the behavior are societal, not individual. Yet the precipitating cause, or those causes most proximate to the individual's actions, must come from the individual. This seems especially true of the relationship between men and women, because it has in part a personal, private aspect.

The phenomenon of antagonism between the sexes is at the same time a psychological phenomenon and a social one. It cannot be explained purely in psychological terms or purely in terms of society. Yet to integrate a theory of the individual's motivation with a theory about society is difficult. We do not know exactly how it happens that individuals in a society may turn out to be motivated in the same ways. It is even difficult to prove that individuals in a society indeed *have* the same motivations, which may be based on unconscious drives, identifications, or conflicts, even though their overt behavior or overt adherence to an ideology may be the same. Unconscious motivations are difficult to ascertain even in one individual, and more so in an aggregate of individuals.

A major difficulty pervades any attempt to address these problems. It is far from clear how to describe the motivation of an individual or of individuals.

Many of the phenomena we are dealing with are subjectively experienced, and therefore difficult for an observer to know or describe. To compound the problem, some of an individual's emotions may be out of his awareness, and may not even be subjectively experienced in a conscious fashion. The emotions subjectively experienced by an individual, which may be the ones which he could report to an observer (if he wished, if he were not inhibited in his report, etc.), may mask the unconscious emotions or in some other way not represent them accurately. Moreover, the individual's subjective feelings may not correspond to an ideology or set of espoused beliefs on the particular subject, generally held by the individual's society. In other words, a conscious expression of belief could mask, in a way unknown to the "believer," an unconscious wish or fear, or a repressed memory or fantasy. Conversely, an individual might also have conscious motivations which he does not express publicly.

We need to distinguish clearly, in dealing with what motivates people to act as they do, whether we mean to be talking about the drives themselves, such as sex and aggression, or the operation of "defense mechanisms" such as repression, reaction formation, sublimation, projection, or denial, or further, the way in which the motivation is manifested in behavior or belief after it has been subjected to defense or other unconscious processes.

We also need better agreement about the order of causation in the relationship between individual psychodynamic processes and societal phenomena. For example, Spiro (4) has suggested that repressions which take place in individuals (such as the repression of in-group aggression in the Sioux) then cause societal phenomena of a certain sort (such as aggressive warfare among the Sioux). Langness (5) on the other hand suggests the reverse order of causation, namely, that societal phenomena, such as the need for residential separation and solidarity for defense in warfare, then cause repressions in the individual, such as, in the Highlands case, a repression of the sex and dependency needs of men toward women (6).

It appears to be very difficult to explain societal behavior in intrapsychic terms, and vice versa, for the reasons just outlined and for others to be taken up later. It is a worthwhile undertaking, but the underlying theories and criteria for explanation are in need of much work. For this reason, and because the psychodynamics of the New Guinea Highlanders have not been studied, my discussion focuses upon observable behavior and commonly espoused ideology, both in the public domain, rather than upon representations of internal psychodynamic or symbolic processes.

II

We might ask what it is that the general study of the typical personality characteristics of New Guinea Highlands men has to do with the relationship between the sexes. We need to examine how men behave in general to see why they might act toward women in certain ways. Men's attitudes toward other people, the way in which they express themselves, the idea they have of their role in society, and the kind of social *persona* they wish to project, are all relevant to their behavior and attitudes toward women.

Men's behavior toward women is more than simply a function of their behavior in general, however. There is a specific orientation of personality and behavior toward women, determined, as I will show later in the chapter, by the structural relationship of men and women. The role of women in production and reproduction, and the role of men in

Socio-Economic Structure and Personality

controlling production and distribution, the socio-political system in which men compete for prestige, the fluctuating nature of political alignment and of group composition, the control exercised by older men, and the prevalence of warfare, among other factors, all give rise to certain behavioral styles, personality characteristics, and ideology.

The personality characteristics of men and women show complementarity. Sometimes the notion of complementarity has been used to suggest that the "fit" between roles or styles of behavior somehow justifies the styles themselves because of their integration as parts of a larger "system." I want to be very careful not to use the notion of complementarity in this sense. Complementarity does not necessarily imply parity, or equality. There is a "fit" between the roles and personality styles of men and women in the Highlands, but the reasons for the "fit" need to be looked at themselves.

Women of the New Guinea Highlands show personality characteristics greatly contrastive to those of men. They are usually retiring and unassuming in public situations. Their demeanor in public is at times so modest, and their eyes so averted (unlike the direct, arrogant stare of forceful men), that they can have a rather downtrodden look. Women's brows are often furrowed, with eyebrows drawn together, and they often look depressed or perplexed. (Interestingly, when women dance at some ceremonials, dressed in their husbands' decorative finery or in objects indicating their husbands' wealth, they sometimes assume the upright bearing and direct gaze of men.)

The personality styles of women and men show complementarity as a function of the complementarity of their structural roles, which we will look at in detail later. Men of the Highlands could not be the way they are if women were very different, or continual fighting between them might ensue.

In this chapter I want to look for some of the causes of the modal or typical personality characteristics of men mentioned at the beginning of the chapter. The argument of the chapter rests on a presumption that needs to be stated clearly. Many of the personality characteristics or styles of behavior, such as flamboyance, narcissism, irascibility, shrewdness, and so forth, appear to be very useful for the social, economic, and political success of an individual man in the Highlands.

We could look at Highland society as posing a set of structural constraints (social, economic, political), each of which constraints may have a degree of freedom or latitude. I am arguing that the particular styles of behavior and of dispositions to behavior (personality characteristics) of Highland men are a response to certain socio-economic constraints in Highland society, as these constraints affect them in adulthood.

Adult personality has traditionally been looked at as a direct result of child rearing and other socialization processes. These are undoubtedly of major importance in the Highlands case as well, as formative influences on the development of modal personality styles. However, there is relatively little information about child rearing in the Highlands, and its lack does not leave much room for explanation.

Whiting (7) has suggested that child rearing practices may sometimes be a response to ecological necessities. For example, a lack of protein in the diet (due to rainy tropical climate) is well correlated cross-culturally with a long nursing period, long post-partum sex taboo, exclusive mother-infant sleeping arrangements, harsh male initiation rituals, and an aggressive masculine style. The New Guinea Highlands (8) data are in good accord with these correlations. Whiting's conclusion that the aggressive masculine style (9) is caused by the need for the young boy or man to differentiate himself from his mother, with whom he has identified too closely during early childhood, seems plausible in the New Guinea Highlands context, though insufficient to account for the range and pervasiveness of the antagonism which characterizes the relationship between men and women.

To explain adult personality only as a result of child rearing practices is rather limiting. Causal relationships are very difficult to determine, and many factors other than socialization may intervene between childhood experience and adult personality.

A formulation such as Whiting's takes the unconscious (which represses the original identification with the mother, and then undergoes a reaction formation which causes excessively "macho" behavior) as the intervening variable, between child rearing and personality. The unconscious, though powerful, does not make a good intervening variable. So little is known about the actual workings of the unconscious that it is extremely difficult to specify the causal mechanism by which the unconscious connects culture-specific child rearing to adult personality.

Even if, for the sake of argument, we assume that adult personality were entirely due to child rearing practices, we would want to know why the child rearing practices in a given society take the form they do. LeVine (10) has suggested that socialization is designed by parents to influence their children to become adults of a certain type, who will function successfully in their society. If there were sufficient information about child rearing in the New Guinea Highlands, it would be very useful to look for the relationships suggested by LeVine. In any case, we would still need to look at the relationship between the socioeconomic structure and the personality characteristics which are necessary for adult "success" within it.

I would argue further that some personality characteristics or styles of behavior are called forth by the socio-economic situation in which adults find themselves, as adults, and that these are not necessarily relevant, or provided for, in childhood or adolesence.

In fact, one of the few studies of child rearing in the Highlands suggests that violence and individualism are not encouraged among children, and that altruism, nurturance, and cooperation on the part of young children are rewarded (11). The discrepancy between the behavior of adults and the behavior of children is all the more striking because the report concerns the Fore, who have been described elsewhere as being among the most self-seeking and aggressive of Highland peoples (12).

Many of the Highland male personality characteristics under discussion may not be called forth in childhood. For example, children may not meet with situations which evince or necessitate behavior such as shrewdness, manipulativeness, or individualism. They may not be rewarded for self-centered or self-aggrandizing behavior. The recent work of Schweder (13) and of Riesman (14) also suggest a discontinuity between traits instilled in childhood and later adult personality.

It is difficult to integrate the unconscious into a theory about society for another reason as well. In speaking about society, we are mostly interested in what people have in common. It is not clear to begin with that the unconscious of an individual resembles those of other individuals in a society, and it is still more unclear how we would know if they did resemble one another. I am not arguing that to know either of these is a logical impossibility, but that the methodology and theory which would enable us to address these problems need to be developed in a coherent way.

When the unconscious is used as an intervening variable in a theory about child rearing, there seems to be an underlying assumption that similar events during socialization, e.g., traumatic experiences such as initiation, or perhaps a similar emphasis on certain psychosexual stages, lead to conflicts, sublimations, repressions, or identifications which are similar among individuals, and that these unconscious mechanisms then cause similarities of personality in the adult members of a society (15).

However, psychoanalytic theory suggests that the configuration of an individual's unconscious is unique, and dependent in subtle ways upon unique events in the individual's history, and that the displacements and condensations of primary process thinking result in an idiosyncratic unconscious symbolic system. It is very hard to generalize about the unconscious (in its manifold workings) of multiple individuals in a given society. The full range of socio-economic-political behavior in which the adult personality finds expression does not seem explainable solely in terms of the unconscious either.

Socialization might also be seen as the total context of childhood experience in which learning styles of behavior takes place. In this sense, a child's observation of the behavior of adults in various contexts would certainly be a formative influence on the development of his or her personality style. Obviously there is some interaction between an individual's experiences during childhood, and an adult personality at a later time which perpetuates certain characteristics for another generation to observe.

But the question here concerns the order of causation we want to employ in explaining the characteristics. One argument, the one more frequently made, is that adult personality results from childhood experiences. I would argue that the process may also operate in reverse: that styles of behavior, even though they may be observed and imitated in childhood, result from factors in adulthood which cause the adult personality a priori to be a certain way. After all, almost any style can be learned in childhood. I want to ask why it is this particular style rather than another.

I am suggesting that adult behavioral style (or personality), when similar among individuals, is similar at least partly because of external constraints and forces on the behavior of adults, from the society's socio-economic organization, and from all of the societal and political ramifications of the form of socio-economic integration.

Following this argument, it is necessary to look at the socio-economic constraints which make certain styles of behavior and personality very useful to men of the Highlands. The general line of my argument is that the structure of the economy and of the society gives rise to a prevailing individualism in the orientation of motivation and behavior, which in turn causes the exaggeration of certain personality characteristics and styles of behavior in men. These directly affect the relationship between men and women.

III

The structure of Highland society fluctuates in membership, loyalty, enmity, and alignment for ceremonial trade and in support of big men. Dissidents may leave and take residence elsewhere (16); fission is a common result of the growth of a successful local group or of friction within the local group (17). At the same time, the societies lack formally constituted authority, institutionalized power, and a mechanism for third-party adjudication.

Due to these factors, and to the professed egalitarian ideology (18), there seems to be only a limited range of means by which a man may gain influence over others. These include asserting himself over others by force of personality and with implied threat, using the power of persuasion and oratory, manipulating the structural arrangements which determine the loyalties of others, manipulating what other people believe, and indebting others to himself in ceremonial exchange. At the same time, the lack of formal authority allows an important degree of latitude for such behavior on the part of individuals, since there is no constituted force to challenge one who has arrogated power to himself.

A pervasive individualism seems to result from the fluidity of Highland social structure, with many ramifications in behavioral style. The composition of the local society as well as the political arrangements within it seem to be more responsive to the actions of individuals than in most societies. Rather than conforming to a kind of Platonic ideal, in which individuals fit into predetermined and relatively fixed social slots, the form itself of society seems to depend on the activities of individuals, particularly of big men.

As we will see below, there is a necessity for individuals to maintain their own sets of ties and relationships, and there may be pronounced conflict between the interests of an individual and the interests of the local group to which he belongs.

Continual competition among local groups for prestige and military success, and among men of a particular locality for prestige, power, and economic success, often make the short-run interests of individuals take precedence over the long-run interests of the society as a whole. The struggle for prestige itself is an important force in orienting behavior, as is the possibility for a man to manipulate social situations to his own advantage. Those most successful in gaining prestige and in manipulating social situations, that is, big men, have an exaggerated version of the personality characteristics shared by most other men.

The importance of the individual man's actions in affecting the arrangement of group composition, cohesion, and sentiment leads to the development of a range of personality characteristics which increase the individual's ability to achieve, maintain, or increase these effects.

The individual's ability to shape the temporary form of society in the Highlands has been noted by several authors. Langness notes that "from the point of view of any individual, many ties with other individuals are possible, only some of which he will choose to maintain. But, from the point of view of formal structural principles, the specific ties cannot be predicted" (19). Barnes suggests that "this multiplicity [of allegiances] in New Guinea is largely a

Socio-Economic Structure and Personality

result of individual initiative and is not due to the automatic operation of rules" (20). Read states that "Gahuku-Gama social groups can only be defined in relative terms, in terms, that is, of some crucial activity in respect of which their members are more closely related amongst themselves than they are with other groups, and this applies not only to the tribes as a whole but also to every segment of whatever order" (21); according to A. Strathern, " ... there is enough play in most Highlands social systems to allow for such individual [alliance] arrangements ... " (22).

On the other hand, Firth has suggested that optation is never unrestricted (23), and Watson suggests that the flux of personnel in local groups may itself be organized (24), that "a social system organizes a flow of personnel in space and time" (25).

These suggestions do raise the possibility that the strength attributed to individual actions in determining social outcomes might be to some degree a problem of description. That is, individual "free choice" might be reinterpretable as a function of some set of social constraints. However, even if the problem can, in a logical sense, be restated in such terms, it is possible that the number of variables simultaneously involved in determining the individual's choice is too great to allow prediction. Certainly the Highlands literature contains no analysis in these terms, which would invalidate the notion that the activities of some individuals seeking their own interests to a large degree determine the social structure, rather than the reverse.

Shifting alignments of group composition and loyalty appear to allow an important degree of latitude for an individual man to turn situations to his own advantage. A. Strathern notes that big men " ... try to extract value out of, and manipulate, marginal situations" (26).

Success in these attempts may lead to control over other members of the society, as well as to control over group composition and the structure of loyalties and debts. I would argue that the potential for success of this kind gives rise to a certain style of personality - shrewd, self-aggrandizing, manipulative, opportunistic, and able to recognize and seize the moment. Even the potential for success, as well as actual success, may be an important force in shaping the style of behavior, for these characteristics must be perfected over time, and lack of success on occasion may not be a deterrent to their development.

Leaders in the Highlands must lead by persuasion and by "force of personality" (27), rather than by formally constituted authority. Men who are not big men are also expected to show qualities of "strength" (28) and to be aggressive and assertive, or risk being labeled "rubbish men." The concept of "strength" of personality seems to translate, at a minimum, into forcefulness of expression, covert threat as to the individual's threshold of tolerance of others' behavior, an appearance of invincibility, and a style of flaunted narcissism.

I would also suggest that, given the complex of Highland social structural features outlined at the beginning of the chapter, a very important means of controlling what people do in the Highlands is by controlling what they think. Several kinds of ideological manipulation can be identified in the Highlands. The use of ambiguity by the local group in the ascription of agnation has been discussed previously. Big men in particular seem to manipulate agnatic ideology to suit their own purposes (29), e.g., in gaining adherents.

The manipulation of others' ideology and sentiments in the Highlands seems to be necessary for economic success as well. Barnes remarks that "In New Guinea a man's capital resources consist largely in the obligations which he has imposed on his partners" (30). Obligations, of course, involve a complex set of sentiments and values. If these are not adhered to consistently by both parties, the obligations rapidly become meaningless (31).

I have argued in an earlier chapter that the ideology concerning the pollutive dangers of women is in part a form of ideological manipulation by older men to control the behavior of younger men, and that women, who are to a large extent controlled by the violence directed against them, are also controlled to a smaller degree by a set of views concerning their personality characteristics. It is interesting to note that from the point of view of an individual man, other men are not controllable through violence to the same degree as women. Consequently, the degree to which manipulation of belief is necessary must be proportionally larger.

The need to control or influence heavily what others think necessitates the development of a certain range of personality characteristics, some of which have already been described. Shrewdness, manipulativeness, and the ability to gauge what others are likely to do in a given situation are also of use. A flamboyant and self-assertive style and a sense of the dramatic may have the effect of convincing others of the worth of an individual's opinions. Reay (32) describes the manner in which a big man voices his opinion: "Commonly, he makes an authoritative pronouncement in a clear commanding voice at a crucial point in public discussion and then turns on his heel to stride away." According to Reay, " ... the greatest development in aesthetic expression is rhetoric" (33).

I encountered a big man among the Wiru people of the Southwestern Highlands whose personality resembled an orchestrated symphony of moods. He greeted my husband and me with a fierce and somber pose, arms crossed and brows drawn. He seized a bow and some arrows and stood staring at us, and then suddenly burst into a gleeful and gracious smile. Afterwards, he joked with us with great charm and humor.

His way of taking control of the situation in which we (who probably seemed to be Australians, the former administrators of the region) had intruded upon his domain was remarkable. He constantly threw us off balance by giving us slightly misleading information and then producing the truth in one form or another immediately afterward. For example, he told my husband (through an interpreter) that there was no such thing as a sacred flute, then produced one from behind his back, laughing, and proceeded to play it with great intensity and seriousness. He pretended that a certain type of shell was worn on the forehead, holding it up to himself in front of the amused village residents. This shell was really supposed to be worn on the chest, as we knew.

Yet his joking with us was never derisive. Later, he was very helpful to us in obtaining some artifacts for a museum. Through his humor one could glimpse a subtle wielding of power by a man who seemed to know exactly what he was doing at every moment. His changeable moods and succession of facial expressions were reminiscent of charismatic and emotive demagogues such as Fidel Castro. In fact, the very changeability itself was an expression of the force of his character and of his position in his own society,

A Sense of Drama in Self-Presentation

because it showed that he had the latitude to set the tone of the encounter.

An exaggeration seems to occur in big men of all of the personality characteristics under discussion, probably as a concomitant of the increased effect of their activities as individuals. The actions of big men are of crucial importance in determining the alignments within the local society and the alliances beyond it. De Lepervanche has suggested, with regard to the activities of big men, that

" ... Big Men in all groups are probably the ultimate decision makers concerning recruitment of non-natal members and ... their role in this respect has been underestimated" (34);
" ... intergroup relations generally are not regulated by the lineage system, but fluctuating states of enmity, amity and neutrality depend to a large extent on the relationships Big Men have with their neighboring peers." (35);
and "The decline of groups in size and status as much as the fluctuation in group composition can be correlated with the pattern of warfare. This in turn depends on the political activities of Big Men and their followers. Growth in size and numbers of local groups also hinges on the ability of leaders to persuade natal-born members to remain and, when land is available, recruits from outside to join. As the size of Highlands groups seems to a large extent to determine their status it would appear, therefore, that Big Men are also instrumental in establishing the autonomy of local units, and their role in the segmentation process is critical" (36).

The ability of a Big Man to persuade or impress, to exert a charismatic pull on his followers and present a charismatic *persona* to other groups, and to serve as a locus for group prestige (37), influences greatly the size, composition, and loyalty of the local group, as well as its standing in intergroup competition for prestige, and to some degree its safety from an outbreak of warfare. It is obvious that an individual in such a situation has much latitude for the expression of his personality, and that the characteristics we have been discussing - flamboyance, narcissism, threatening demeanor, opportunism, and so forth - are well suited to charismatic leadership and to the manipulation of group structure.

There is another effect of the actions of big men which must be taken into account as well. The actions of big men are self-serving in the short run, yet they affect the form of the entire society in the long run. For example, a big man's drive to gain supporters in local factionalism, and his consequent recruitment of new individuals to the local group, may not in some instances be beneficial to the local society as a whole. Moreover, other people of the local group may have some short-run interests allied with those of a particular big man, and because their short-run interests are dependent upon his success, they may act in certain ways which may not be consonant with their own long-run interests. Consequently, there may be a continual skewing of social organization in the direction of what is in the short-run interests of individuals rather than in the long-run interests of society.

The potential for structural contradiction between the interests of individuals and those of the local society seems to be pronounced in the Highlands. For example, Hayano notes that "On an individual basis ... men are making political decisions regarding their own and village security as the top priority in preference to most extra-village obligations and affinal responsibilities" (38). However, since individuals, in seeking their own security, may make use of their own ties with members of other groups (39), and may find it advantageous to flee an area rather than to defend it, it seems likely that the security of an individual may in some cases conflict with the security of the local group to which he is attached.

The necessity for the individual to maintain his own set of ties seems to be generated by a number of factors, including the fluctuating nature of group composition, the potential need to take refuge in warfare, and the demands of ceremonial exchange. The maintenance of these individual ties in turn sets up a situation in which there may be conflict between the interests of the individual and those of the local group to which he belongs. Both the maintenance of the ties and the structural contradiction generated by them probably encourage the self-seeking individualism which has been widely reported in the Highlands. According to Berndt (40), "... emphasis ... is placed on individual achievement, even, in extreme cases, at the expense of close patri-kin."

Socio-Economic Structure and Personality

The process of competition itself (apart from whatever is being competed for) may exacerbate the development of the personality characteristics and behavior under discussion. Continual competition exists among surrounding groups of a locality, even among allies, and among men of a particular locality, for prestige, political support, and success in ceremonial exchange, and in some cases for military success and conquest of land (41). A. Strathern notes that:

> " ... Highland societies were in the recent past subject to vigorous ongoing processes of competition ... over a span of several hundred years these processes of competition may have both engendered and been facilitated by continual expansion and movement of Highlands populations over the entire area which they currently occupy. Possibly the availability of areas for expansion fostered continual replication of the feature of structural open-ness ... " (42).

I would suggest that the forces of competition pose a very strong selective pressure for decisions to be made in the short run interests of individuals, rather than in the long-run interests of society, or even in some cases in the long-run interests of those individuals. That is, actions may be undertaken for the sake of expediency in competition which would not otherwise be undertaken. (A parallel might be drawn with the evolution of the human vertebral column, which, because of the very great selective pressure for upright posture, took place too rapidly for the details of the vertebral structure to be perfected.) Over time, the society as a whole becomes structured by the effects of a series of self-interested decisions.

It seems likely that since big men and aspiring big men succeed in competition with one another (43), there may be a continual escalation of what is necessary for success, and a concomitant exaggeration of the personality characteristics outlined above. The concept of schizmogenesis, first developed by Bateson in analyzing the Iatmul of the Sepik region, is relevant in this regard. Bateson was primarily interested in the differentiation of sex roles, which he believed was due to schizmogenesis, defined as "a process of differentiation in the norms of individual behavior resulting from cumulative interaction between individuals"

(45). We can also use the notion of schizmogenesis here, to suggest that individuals, or sets of individuals, may mutually exaggerate their behavior in response to the reactions of the other set of individuals to previous behavior.

IV

There are a number of other factors involved in the generation of the male Highlander's personality and the expression of personality toward women and other individuals, having generally to do with the competition for prestige and power in Highland societies.

The fluctuating character of political alignment, membership, and exchange relationship in Highland societies, described previously, gives rise to a situation in which all status is achieved, in which there is a continual struggle for power and prestige among men of the local group, and in which there is a continual arrogation, or potential arrogation, of power over others by some individuals.

I would argue that this situation in turn causes a certain type of social interaction, which has been widely described, but not explained, in the Highlands.

Although competition for prestige, often presented as an end in itself or as an alternative satisfaction to material gain, is widely reported to be an extremely important motivation for behavior in the Highlands (46), just what "prestige" really is, and the processes by which it operates to confer power and organize behavior have not been given much attention.

The concept of prestige comes from our own society, where it also figures importantly as a motivation for behavior; perhaps its centrality in our own culture makes it hard for us to look behind its apparent meaning. But it is a slippery notion even in our own societal context (47), implying social consensus yet difficult to define or measure, or to assess the way in which it is allocated. Its meaning in the Highlands context ought not to be taken for granted. I have treated these problems at length elsewhere (48). Here I focus only upon the aspects of the struggle for prestige which bear directly upon the relationship between the sexes.

In a situation of continual realignment, rising and declining leadership, and actual or potential arrogation of power, it seems likely that people very often do not know exactly where they stand relative to other members of the local society. Moreover, relative position in the Highlands is communicated not by individuals occupying a pre-existing hierarchical relationship, but seemingly by more subtle manifestations of deference on the one hand and intractability on the other. Big men seem to have license to break the rules (49), and other men also gain prestige by being belligerent and argumentative. Reay, for example, states that "It is not particularly rewarding for a man to keep out of quarrels: for the most he can expect to achieve by conforming closely with the rules is a kind of anonymity in a society that values renown" (50). According to Berndt, "It is by asserting himself against others, making them do what he wants or doing what he wants with them, that a man shows himself to be 'strong.' In choosing action to bring about the consequences he desires, he may go contrary to socially accepted rules ... " (51).

Conversely, an individual loses prestige through quiet acceptance of others' affronts to himself. Hayano notes that "a man can choose not to settle or prosecute ... [an] offense; men who do this are insulted and regarded as cowards" (52).

The individual man must act in an aggressive and defensive manner in order to avoid being taken advantage of by others; big men must act in a high-handed manner to avoid being superseded (53). Continual revalidation of position is required (54), and necessitates continual attention to subtle indications of others' conceptions of the individual's relative standing. I would argue that these factors explain in large measure the hypersensitivity to insult and extreme concern with defense of reputation (55), and the need to demonstrate forcefulness of personality, widely reported for the Highlands area.

In such a situation, it is important to maintain not only real invincibility, which must be tested directly, but also the appearance of invincibility, communicated in terms of potential threat (56). The treatment of women seems to be an important means of publicly demonstrating irascibility, the potential for violence, and the threshold of tolerance for others' behavior. Brutality toward women may be a kind of implied threat toward other men. Women are particularly opportune subjects for display of this kind because, being unimportant politically, they are also politically neutral; that is, the way they are treated has few adverse repercussions on the relationships among men of the local group. Being defenseless, women are also unable to reciprocate.

Denitch has suggested, in regard to the Balkans, that the need to project a unified and apparently invulnerable front to feuding enemy groups leads men to control stringently the behavior of in-marrying wives. The affront to the "'honor'" (57) of a Balkans group when a woman publicly contravenes the authority of male affines has a parallel in the loss of prestige to a New Guinea Highlands man who is publicly unable to control his wife or wives. M. Strathern, for example, states that "The wife rather than the husband usually gains most in publicizing a grievance, for the male image of the latter is of one who controls his wives and settles disputes internally, and does indeed have authority over them" (58).

That men may communicate with one another through their behavior toward women receives some fragmentary support in the literature. M. Strathern notes that a wife "may have been back and forth with requests over the matter [unreciprocated ceremonial exchange], and had to bear the brunt of the husband's annoyance. Ashamed himself to show anger toward his in-laws, he upbraids his wife for the relatives she has" (59). Koch states that " ... the agnates of a woman whom her husband beats for nothing when it was he who last equalized the balance [in ceremonial exchange], may interpret his conduct as conferring a request for a *hoptoxo* [pertaining to ceremonial exchange] pig" (60). According to Read, "A youth ... who neglects the rules of avoidance which are enjoined during his betrothal is considered to have affronted his age mates, who may retaliate by killing the girl he expects to become his wife" (61). Watson notes, with regard to a despotic big man, that "Matoto's open freedom with other men's wives, whether or not it had an appreciable libidinous component, ... the violation of other men's rights, the offense against mores, and the wanton disregard of all the conventional cautions about male strength and female sexuality ... were just what they were meant to be. They established Matoto's immunity to ordinary restrictions, to the rules that inhibited ordinary men" (62).

There are several other respects in which the competition for prestige and power among men bears upon the relationship between the sexes. The operation of prestige necessarily implies an audience with shared values as to what is prestigious. It is not generally very clear in the Highlands literature whether the audience for prestige, which only men may possess, is limited to men, or whether the audience includes both men and women. However, we might deduce that the intended (at least the overtly intended) audience for prestige is male, because most of the material, social, and political ramifications of increased prestige depend upon the actions of other men. That is, military allies, trade partners, and political supporters, all of whom are men, become more numerous as a function of increased prestige.

Success in ceremonial trade causes a self-generating increase, in geometric progression. Success inspires confidence on the part of potential trade partners that debts will be repaid and equal gifts returned, and these partners consequently seek to trade with the successful individual. Increased prestige, dependent upon success in ceremonial trade, also attracts military allies (63), and may act importantly as a threat to potentially belligerent groups, deterring them from attack (64).

Increased prestige may bring greater success in attracting marital and other female sexual partners, but this is sometimes the result of other men proffering their sisters or daughters in order to gain a wealthy or powerful affine and exchange partner (65), rather than because of free choice on the part of women. Interestingly, under the limited circumstances, such as courting parties, when women may exercise choice, or when they make an unsanctioned choice, as in elopement, women seem to choose men on the basis of their physical attractiveness, not their prestige gained through political or economic activity (66). In some societies young men take pains to make themselves more attractive to women (67).

Men are at least overtly the intended audience for prestige in another respect as well. The opinions of women are generally disregarded and devalued, and consequently it would be inconsistent for men to compete openly for their approval. It is possible, though, that women may be an unconsciously intended audience for masculine display.

According to Berndt, "In one sense women provide a background against which men can highlight their own achievements, a foil for their display of 'strength.' The contrast itself appears to stimulate men and enhance their sense of self-esteem ... " (68).

Interestingly, in view of the general devaluation of women, success with sexual partners is reported to be a source of prestige for men (69), but the audience for the prestige is probably other men, because boasting about sexual exploits usually takes place in the men's house, in the exclusive company of men (70). Moreover, women are angered rather than impressed by the philandering of men (71), and it is therefore unlikely that they consider such behavior to be desirable or prestigious.

Men compete for one another's approval, yet in order to reach the goals which confer prestige, they are critically dependent in most respects upon the activities of women (72). Wives produce the *sine qua non* of ceremonial exchange, namely pigs, and success in ceremonial exchange is the major source of prestige. Consequently, men control the behavior of women not only because of hostility, but also because they are dependent upon the actions of women for the approval and political support of men, and in fact for their standing in the community. What is at first sight a struggle for control between men and women, therefore, must be interpreted in terms of a struggle, through prestige and the political support which it brings about, among men themselves.

The fact that only some (men), and not others (women), may have prestige, delimits the legitimate contenders for power and renders women politically irrelevant (73). Even if women were able to gain a measure of control, for example in the allocation of goods which they had produced (74), the fact that prestige cannot be ascribed to them effectively removes them from the political arena.

Mary Douglas has suggested (75) that prestige goods may be used as rationing coupons for the licensing of social status. In a similar way, the very possibility of the ascription of prestige itself may be used to define social statuses and who may occupy them.

In summary, we can see that men's behavior toward women must be looked at in the context of the struggle for prestige and power among men, as a communicatory device, and as part of the expression of personality characteristics developed in response to the system of wealth accumulation and in response to the unstable social structure of Highland societies.

Notes - Chapter Four

1. Read 1954a:5-6; Reay 1959a:191-193; Berndt 1962:173-174; Newman 1964b:16; Langness 1965:277.
2. Several studies using techniques such as projective testing (Poole 1982:102), dream elicitation, and life history (Poole ibid.; Herdt 1981; 1982) have been undertaken in New Guinea groups outside the Highlands, but there have been none in the Highlands per se. Herdt (ibid.) has investigated the psychological aspect of cultural symbols in his study of ritualized homosexuality and its subjective meaning among the Sambia. But among the Highlanders, who do not have ritualized or otherwise socially acceptable homosexuality (Herdt 1984:41-43), psychodynamic integration and development must be considerably different.
3. LeVine (1973:Chapters 5, 12-14) and Kracke (1980) have discussed these problems at length.
4. Spiro 1961:110-114.
5. Langness 1976b:163.
6. Keesing (1982), Herdt (1982), and Read (1982:69) have also linked male initiation rites to the necessity to make "warriors" of men.
7. Whiting 1969.
8. The New Guinea Highlands, although equatorial in latitude, have a Marine West Coast climate, rather than a strictly tropical one.
9. J. Whiting, R. Kluckhohn, and A. Anthony 1958; Burton and J. Whiting 1961; B. Whiting 1965; J. Whiting and B. Whiting 1975.
10. LeVine 1973:128,133.
11. Sorenson 1976:182-189.
12. Berndt 1962.
13. Schweder 1979:272-275.
14. Riesman n.d. See also Wolfenstein 1955:114-116.
15. Herdt, for example (1981; 1982:49,51), suggests that an "intersubjective fantasy system" regarding the symbolism of flutes "derives from subjective meanings based on individual developmental experience." The notion of an intersubjective fantasy system raises some puzzling philosophical issues.
16. Watson 1970:120-121.
17. de Lepervanche 1968:180, citing evidence regarding the Kuma, Kyaka, Mae Enga, Mendi, and Bena Bena.

18. Berndt 1962:416; Ryan 1969:170; Sillitoe 1979:5; Feil 1980:27-28; Josephides 1983:302.
19. Langness 1969:52.
20. Barnes 1962:7.
21. Read 1954a:42.
22. A. Strathern 1969a:49.
23. quoted in A. Strathern 1972:216.
24. Watson 1970:110-111.
25. ibid:108. Watson does not define the size or structure of the unit to be considered a system, however, or demonstrate that the local society is a "system."
26. A. Strathern 1972:228.
27. Newman 1965:44; Berndt 1969:358; Rappaport 1968:29; Brandewie 1971:202.
28. Berndt 1962:173.
29. de Lepervanche 1967:151; 1968:183-184; A. Strathern 1972:221, 228-229.
30. Barnes 1962:8.
31. Sillitoe argues that exchange is the major force in Wola (Southern Highlands) society which constrains self-interested behavior and directs it toward the good of society (1979:160,170,283,288,290), and that exchange in fact developed to "facilitate cooperation and harmony in social life" (ibid:23).
32. Reay 1959a:117.
33. ibid:193.
34. De Lepervanche 1968:176.
35. ibid:178.
36. ibid: 179.
37. M. Strathern 1978:177,199.
38. Hayano 1974:289-290.
39. Langness 1969:54; Rappaport 1969:121.
40. Berndt 1962:398.
41. cf. de Lepervanche 1968:181-182.
42. A. Strathern 1972:230.
43. de Lepervanche 1968:176.
44. Bateson 1958: Chapter 13.
45. ibid:175.
46. e.g., Elkin 1953:197; Salisbury 1962:199; Pospisil 1963b:392; de Lepervanche 1968:177; Meggitt 1967:31; Berndt 1969:337; A. Strathern 1971c:2; Feil 1980:35.
47. Interestingly, the original meaning of the word "prestige" in English was "illusion, a conjuring trick, deception, imposture," deriving from 16th c. French and ultimately Latin words which also meant illusion or delusion, or juggler's tricks (Oxford English Dictionary: 1322). "Charisma" and "glamour" are also derived from earlier words with connotations of magic or mystery.
48. Gelber n.d.

49. Read 1959:434; Watson 1967b:68; Lowman-Vayda 1968:215; Berndt 1969:338; Meggitt 1974:191.
50. Reay 1959a:123.
51. Berndt 1962:398.
52. Hayano 1974:285.
53. Berndt 1969:358.
54. de Lepervanche 1968:182.
55. e.g., Read 1954a:23; Reay 1959a:125-126; Meggitt 1965a:179; M. Strathern 1972:339.
56. cf. Collier and Rosaldo (1981:294) on the use of violence or potential violence to maintain equality among in-marrying men of uxorilocal hunter-gatherer and hunter-horticulturalist societies.
57. Denitch 1974:255.
58. M. Strathern 1972:276.
59. ibid:130.
60. Koch 1968a:104.
61. Read 1954a:23.
62. Watson 1967b:78.
63. Bulmer 1960:12.
64. Meggitt 1974:171; Josephides 1985:143. Healey (1978) suggests that the elaboration of ceremonial exchange, with its concomitant emphasis on prestige, serves to create and reinforce the alliance relations needed in warfare (particularly in areas of greater population pressure).
65. Watson 1967b:74.
66. Reay 1959a:22,176; Bowers 1965:36; Langness 1967b:172; Lowman-Vayda 1968:208; Cook 1969:101; Ryan 1969:164.
67. Cook ibid; A. Strathern and M. Strathern 1971:126; Langness 1974:198.
68. Berndt 1962:403.
69. Reay 1959a:169; Berndt 1962:151,157; Langness 1969:45.
70. Reay ibid.; Gillison 1980:153.
71. Reay 1959a:82; Berndt 1962:128.
72. cf. Langness 1974:205.
73. M. Strathern (1978) suggests that although women among the Melpa may be accorded some prestige for aiding men with their endeavors (ibid:184), they are thought of in that case as being like men (ibid:187,188), so that, as she puts it, "to achieve at all is to be male" (ibid:186).
74. M. Strathern 1972: Chap. 6.
75. Douglas 1967a:129.

*"You'd be bored.
Birth and copulation and death:
That's all the facts when you come to brass tacks."*
T. S. Eliot, "Sweeney Agonistes."

5

Aversion Toward Women as a Population Regulatory Device

I

Is the fear of women as a source of pollution a method of birth control, which limits the size of the population? Several authorities on the New Guinea Highlands have made this intriguing suggestion.

For example, Lindenbaum states that " ... In societies where available resources are endangered by further population increase ... fear of pollution is a form of ideological birth control ... Belief in the contaminating powers of women, together with certain socially accepted behavioral manipulations, appears to have resulted in an effective barrier to human reproduction" (1). Sanday (2) espouses this conclusion and incorporates it into a more extensive argument about the relationship between the kind of food supply and the fear of pollution from sexual relations.

Glasse, in a similar way, suggests that the simultaneous ideological stress on fertility and chastity for men among the Huli can be explained as "alternative reproductive strategies employed respectively in times of abundant soil productivity due to sporadic volcanic ash falls, and in lean times due to drought, frost or excessive rainfall" (3).

Bulmer states that "It is possible that culturally conditioned restraints on enthusiasm for heterosexual intercourse, expressed in many New Guinea societies as a fear that female contamination will sap the strength of the male, may have some effect on fertility, though as far as I am aware there is no good evidence to demonstrate this" (4), but he concludes by citing data (regarding the ratio of pregnancy to acts of coitus) which he says "suggests that any diminution of frequency of intercourse may restrict fertility" (5).

The idea that women are dangerously polluting, especially while menstruating, and that sexual contact is debilitating, is a pervasive one in the Highlands. For example, Meggitt says that the Mae Enga believe that "copulation is in itself detrimental to male well-being ... Overindulgence must dull his mind and leave his body permanently exhausted and withered" (6), and that "contact ... with a menstruating woman will ... sicken a man and cause persistent vomiting, turn his blood black, corrupt his vital juices so that his skin darkens as his flesh wastes, permanently dull his wits, and eventually lead to a slow decline and death" (7). Similar beliefs are reported for the Kamano and Fore (8), the Melpa (9), the Gururumba (10), and the Gahuka-Gama (11), among others.

The idea that aversion toward women can be explained as a form of population regulation is interesting and at first sight seems creditable. But what is really necessary in order to give an explanation of this kind? It is useful to examine in a fair amount of detail the complexity of factors which may be involved in giving an anthropological explanation, using this hypothesis as a case in point. My intention is to question both the specific suggestion and some of the assumptions on which it is dependent, with the aim of making clearer how far one must sometimes go in order to assess the truth, validity, or usefulness of a hypothesis.

In particular, I wish to bring out the premises and presuppositions which remain tacit in the argument. Every explanation is founded upon premises which leave some things unexplained, even though these things may themselves be subjects for examination by another branch of science. Even if it is not reasonable to question every premise, it is important to bring to light what the premises are, to be aware explicitly of what is being left as an assumption, and to question those premises which set the meaning of the terms used in the explanation, or in which the meaning might be ambiguous. Confusions can often be resolved when the meaning of the terms used in a hypothesis are explored and delimited. Meaning in a scientific context ought to be denotative, saying only one thing at a time (and not connotative, as it is in a literary context, making use of the various associations that words may suggest or evoke).

In this chapter and the next I want to unravel the suggestion that the fear of women acts to regulate population size, to see the strands of meaning and argument which are involved in proving or disproving such a suggestion. My examination takes the form of assessing the evidence for population pressure in the New Guinea Highlands, and of discussing some of the problems which arise in giving evidence for population pressure. Then, assuming for the sake of argument that there is population pressure, I discuss whether *horror mulieris* (aversion, fear, and disgust toward women) would in fact control the population size. Finally, I criticize some aspects of explanation given in ecological terms, particularly the notion of adaptation, since these aspects are crucial to the validity of an explanation given in terms of population pressure.

II

The evidence for population pressure in the Highlands comes from several sources. According to Watson, the introduction of the sweet potato (Ipomoea batatas), a New World plant, into the Highlands about three hundred years ago caused "a subsistence revolution" (12), and as a result, "a late explosive growth of population" (13). The use of the sweet potato as a subsistence crop allowed the expansion of populations into higher altitude, formerly unoccupied, territory where it had not been possible previously to grow subsistence crops. According to Watson, the sweet potato was the first crop to be intensively and sedentarily cultivated in the Highlands (14). Bulmer and Bulmer (15) present supporting evidence, and Sorenson (16) is in agreement, although according to Brookfield (17), taro may have been intensively cultivated before the introduction of the sweet potato. Brookfield agrees, however, that the sweet potato allowed expansion into higher altitudes to take place (18).

It seems possible that the rapid growth of population and continual expansion into new areas might have created a situation in which a dramatic means of population control would be required when the group reached the limits of expansion. If this limitation of expansion occurred in the recent past, the old forms of behavior leading to population expansion might have proved inadequate, and the general antagonism and confusion resulting from such social dislocation might have been focused upon the relationship between procreators.

There is much evidence that Highland groups have stringent altitudinal limits for settlement, both upper and lower, and that there are therefore well-defined limits to the area in which population can expand. Brookfield describes the area of settlement as a "narrow and broken altitudinal band, sharply limited both above and below" (19). The lower limits of occupation are set chiefly by the prevalence of malaria in the lower altitudes (20), as well as by grasslands degraded, from formerly productive lands, by human occupation (21), and by the indefensibility of low-lying ground (22). The upper limits are set by occasional frost, persistent cloud cover, low temperatures, or excessive rainfall (23), or by a combination of these factors. Brookfield reports that sixty percent of Highland people live between five thousand and six thousand feet, and most of the remainder between six thousand and seven thousand feet (24).

In addition to land needed for the cultivation of human food and pig fodder, land is also needed for fallowing, for pig grazing (25), and for a "no-man's land" to form a boundary between inimical groups (26). It is obvious, therefore, that there are limits to the resources of the Highlands and that there are complex demands upon these resources.

There are other indices of possible population pressure as well. Protein malnutrition in the Highlands has been reported by a number of authors (27), in some cases severe (28). Even where the protein intake has been reported as "probably adequate for everyday activities" (29), in an area with greater sources of vegetable protein than most (30) and a relatively low population density (31), the author has suggested that "it may be less than adequate in stress situations" (32).

Pressure on land resources for some groups is suggested by the fact that land conquest is an explicit aim of warfare for those groups, for example, the Enga (33), Chimbu (34), and Fore (35).

On the other hand, other groups do not fight over land, for example, the Kuma (36), or are reported to "feel ... that every man has more land than he needs" (37). According to Bulmer, "There is in New Guinea ... little evidence of deliberate attempts to limit family size either because of consciousness of general over-population in relation to land and food resources or because of pressure on land available to the individual family or local kin group" (38). Sillitoe concludes that the correlation between population densities for various groups in New Guinea, and the existence of warfare over land in those groups, is weak, but I find the correlation between his categories somewhat more convincing than he seems to himself (39).

The problem of assessing pressure on land and other resources is an extremely complicated one, however. Brown and Podolefsky (40) comment on the difficulties involved in comparing the population densities, as measured by different researchers, of different groups in the Highlands. Complex factors are also involved in determining pressure on land resources, including the various uses to which land must be put, mentioned above, and such factors as mode of cultivation, soils, climatic factors, nutrient composition of crops, length of fallowing periods, and per capita land holdings (41), and the size of the pig herd to be maintained (42).

Similarly, the size of a human population should not be treated as a simple function of available resources, adjusting itself in an invariant way to an inflexible carrying capacity. For example, among the Chimbu, the use of intensive agricultural methods has increased as the population has increased in the last forty years (43), but it seems to have led to land degradation, such as land slips and exposed subsoil (44). Significantly, increased population has nonetheless not caused a reduction of fertility among the Chimbu (45), but has led to a lower caloric intake per capita (40% lower energy intake for adult males and females in 1975 than in 1956) (46).

The notion of carrying capacity, which is essential to any argument concerning pressure on resources, also poses many theoretical difficulties. Carrying capacity has been defined as "the maximum population density the system is capable of supporting permanently in that environment without damage to the land" (47).

Some of the problems which the concept of carrying capacity poses are practical ones. As Clarke points out, assessing land degradation is not a simple matter, because most studies are synchronic and do not take account of new tools, crops, and techniques which may be introduced, changes in the nutritive value or quantity of crops, and cumulative land deterioration (48). The assessment of population pressure is always dependent on the technology available in the area for food production and other forms of energy capture. Brush (49) points out in a similar way that the acreage needed per capita has many determinants, each of them involving a set of variables with a wide range of values. For example, the factor of cropping methods alone (50) has numerous components, each of which can change the potential output.

The practical problems associated with the enumeration and quantification of aggregate resources, and the difficulty of identifying a single limiting factor (51), as well as the problem of assessing the point at which environmental degradation begins (52), are considered so unsurmountable by Dewar that he concludes that "there is little place in anthropology for Cc" as a regulator of population size (53). (Cc is defined by Dewar as "the productive capacity of the environment divided by the per capita requirements of a human population" (54).)

Although Dewar very usefully points out a number of interesting problems and assumptions concerning carrying capacity (55), I would argue that we need to distinguish between *practical* problems in a theory and logically puzzling or insolvable ones. The existence of pragmatic problems is not sufficient cause to abandon ecosystemic regulation as a major determinant of human population size, since the theory itself has not been shown to have an inconsistent structure.

In place of environmental productivity as the prime regulator of population size, Dewar suggests that maximum size is determined by "an unspecified number of density-dependent effects spanning a wide range of proximate causes" (56). However, he does not detail the mechanism by which density dependence might regulate population size, nor specify how the upper limit of population size (which should determine the maximum density) is itself determined (57), and it is difficult to translate his suggestions into a program for analysis.

One specific suggestion which Dewar makes regarding the effect of density dependence on population size is that the density of local populations in a region may be equalized by migration among them (58). Kelly makes a similar observation with regard to the New Guinea Highlands: that population pressure in a given area must also be defined in terms of the population-redistributive methods of the societies involved (59). In the New Guinea Highlands these would include fission, routing in warfare, adoption, recruiting or admitting new adult members, and differential marriage rates among groups.

Another problem is that there are different methods of assessing carrying capacity for groups practicing shifting cultivation, such as those developed by Allan (60), Carneiro (61), and Conklin (62), each of which yields a different result from the same data.

But the most difficult problems inherent in the notion of carrying capacity are those having to do with the meaning of the terms used in talking about carrying capacity and with the use to which the concept of carrying capacity is put in explanation.

Although carrying capacity is usually defined in terms of a maximum population supportable in a given environment (and with a given technology), the actual populations of areas which have been studied in the New Guinea Highlands all seem to be below the carrying capacity as determined by one or another of the formulae, sometimes far below. For example, the Siane are at "somewhat less than 50% of carrying capacity" (63), the Chimbu groups on the average at 60% (64), and the Tsembaga Maring at "well below the carrying capacity of their territory" (65) - using Rappaport's method of estimating mean carrying capacity (66), the calculated figure would be 56%. The Wola, with twice the population density of the Maring, have only 2.04% of their territory under cultivation, and 50% of their territory under primary forest (67).

Moreover, these low percentages are apparently not an accident, according to some theories about population regulation. Wynne-Edwards, while agreeing that "Darwin was undoubtedly right in concluding that food is the factor that normally puts an extreme limit on population density" (68), says nonetheless that " ... the link between food productivity and population density is very far from self-evident. The relationship between them does not typically involve any signs of undernourishment" (69). Similarly, Hayden, in an article focusing on mechanisms of population regulation, says that "It shall ... be taken as a valid assumption that ... the vast majority of hunter/gatherer populations are and were maintained well below carrying capacity" (70). Vayda, in a similar vein, argues that warfare over land can begin long before a group reaches carrying capacity (71).

The assumptions seem to make the notion of carrying capacity somewhat irrelevant. If all groups are assumed to maintain themselves significantly below carrying capacity, how are we to distinguish between those which are motivated by pressure on resources and those which are not? If it is assumed that they are all motivated by population pressure, how can this be demonstrated? How can it be shown that any of them is pressing on resources, or that pressure on resources can be used to explain societal phenomena? For example, if they are all "well below carrying capacity," why do some groups fight over land and not others?

It has been suggested, however, that there are homeostatic mechanisms which maintain the population below carrying capacity. The society, human or animal, is assumed to take as an index of population pressure some factor or factors, which set a lower limit to population than the carrying capacity, and to adjust itself in number to this factor (72).

Although this is not the place for a full-scale examination of the suggestion, we could note some of the problems which it poses. It is not clear in what terms the suggestion may be proven or disproven. The criteria for determining what the optimum level of population might be are not obvious. Is one level better than another? If not, why is homeostasis necessary?

What are the factors which cause a population to be maintained at a certain percentage of carrying capacity, rather than another? If carrying capacity is not a direct influence, is any level of population below carrying capacity to be interpreted as the optimum? What factors or types of factors may act as indices of pressure, and hence as homeostatic regulators, below the carrying capacity? The answers to these questions are crucial for the strengthening of ecological explanation, which is partially dependent upon the notion of carrying capacity.

Some light is shed on these questions by the recent work of Hassan (73); his work in turn raises other questions. He makes a distinction between the maximum, critical, and optimum carrying capacity. Noting that the actual population size of hunter-gatherers and swidden horticulturalists is 20-60% of the average short-term estimate of carrying capacity (74), he calls these short-term estimates "inflated" and says that they "measure a maximum carrying capacity" and are "based on short-term observations during favorable periods" (75), but he does not say why he believes the observations to have been made during favorable periods, nor why being based on short-term observation should influence the estimates upward. On a random basis, neither of these is expectable. It does matter whether the estimates are inflated or not, because what we are trying to get at here is the indeterminate quality of our understanding about the relationship between resources and population size.

Hassan suggests that estimates of critical carrying capacity take into consideration the fluctuation of resources, including those which are critical for nutrition, and that "critical carrying capacity is not exactly equivalent to the actual average population over a long period ... populations cushion themselves against occasional severe shortages or stochastic population fluctuations by existing below the critical carrying capacity at ... the optimum carrying capacity" (76). He further suggests that a population avoids nearing the critical carrying capacity by limiting its size in response to perceived "cues of environmental resistance" (77), or in response to a lowering of the standard of living, such as "scarcity of choice food items, increase in work load per producer, or need to travel further or reschedule subsistence activities differently" (78).

Although Hassan's useful distinction between optimum and critical carrying capacity helps to clarify the relationship between the actual population size and the apparent maximum carrying capacity, as measured by swidden agriculture experts, the mechanism by which "optimum carrying capacity" is maintained remains problematic.

Hassan's model presupposes that a subjectively experienced drop in the standard of living motivates more or less conscious population control by individuals. Conscious control of fertility of this kind involves a complex set of decisions, made by individuals year by year, in response to changes in their perceived mode of life - rather as educated urban dwellers of the post-industrialized West might do. It is not at all clear that people in smaller scale and technologically less sophisticated societies perceive their options, or the relationship between their actions and the quality of their lives, in quite the same existential way as "modern" practitioners of contraception, nor that they have the means available to them to do so.

Moreover, Hassan's model presupposes that the feedback from control of fertility is apparent to the practitioners, and that they themselves experience some benefit from avoided births. Yet neither of these is necessarily the case. His argument assumes that what benefits the individual in fertility (number of offspring) also benefits the collectivity in overall population size, and vice versa. However, research has shown that individuals may benefit from larger numbers of offspring even when the society as a whole is too large for the available resources (79).

Finally, there is a considerable time lag between the actions taken to control the fertility of individuals and the effects on the overall population size (between one and nine generations according to Hassan) (80). There would perhaps be an even greater time lag before the benefits became apparent to the members of society, who by that time would not even be the same individuals who had originally limited their fertility.

Consequently, it seems that individuals left to their own perceptions of environmental stress will have insufficient information and feedback on which to base their decisions, and that *cultural* prescriptions and proscriptions regarding family size and child spacing are necessary to constrain individual decision making.

Yet here we have returned to the original problem: what perpetuates cultural notions which restrict fertility? If they are "adaptive," how are they selected for? How does it happen that people constrain their reproduction in accordance with what is better for the society than, in some cases, for themselves?

There are other serious problems involved in specifying pressure on resources and the optimum level of population, as well. A set of desiderata (at the least, a covert set) for the population are implied in setting a maximum level of population. There must always be a trade-off between the size, health and quality of life of individuals on the one hand, and the absolute number of individuals on the other. In other words, the notion of "supporting" a number of individuals (up to a "maximum") includes some implicit criteria for what constitutes "support," which need to be more clearly specified than they have been previously.

A related problem is that it is possible to be overpopulated with respect to one resource and underpopulated with respect to another (81), although the use of a limiting factor in the analysis may help to resolve this difficulty. It is also possible that different population densities are needed for different critical requirements of the group, and that they may even be in conflict with one another. For example, it seems probable that the optimum population for defense in a New Guinea Highlands group is different from the optimum population vis à vis food resources, and that this contradiction may generate tensions in the social structure. In talking about an optimum, it is crucial that we phrase it in terms of certain desiderata to be maximized, since there may be several desiderata critical to the society whose maximizations are in conflict.

Another major problem in assessing pressure on resources concerns the degree to which we take as relevant the opinion of the group under study, or whether we assume that they act under pressures of which they are unconscious. This problem assumes particular importance because nearly all groups in the New Guinea Highlands on whom data are available seem to operate far below carrying capacity. Therefore, immediate pressure on resources cannot be taken as the motivation which precipitates their behavior, even if it may be an underlying cause. Yet some groups reportedly feel that they have enough land, for example, while others do not. It is, of course, possible that some groups operate much further below carrying capacity than others, and are therefore less aware of pressure on resources, but conflicting information makes it hard to draw a conclusion.

Oddly enough, one of the few groups for which detailed carrying capacity and population density information is available, and which is reported *not* to feel pressure on land resources (82), approaches carrying capacity more closely than any other. In contradiction to the rest of the data concerning population levels vis à vis carrying capacity, this society is estimated by Conklin's formula to be four persons short of carrying capacity (83), or at 97.4% of carrying capacity; or by Carneiro's formula, 44 persons short of carrying capacity (84), or at 77.7% of carrying capacity.

Some authors have maintained that the subjective impressions of the people under study regarding presumably scarce resources and population pressure are not relevant to the assessment of population pressure (85), while other authors seem to have taken these impressions as a very important criterion for the assessment of population pressure, or lack of it (86). This is obviously a very serious, though not much discussed, difference in methodological procedure. One author has argued that in order for the regulatory mechanisms to work, it is essential that the people themselves not understand the functioning of the mechanisms (87). On the other hand, as we have seen, Hassan seems to take conscious assessment of the relationship between population size and standard of living, and conscious control of fertility, as the *sine qua non* of his argument.

Rappaport takes a moderate stand, saying that "the operation of ritual as a regulating mechanism is not necessarily understood by the Tsembaga ... it would be possible to elucidate the regulatory functions of Tsembaga ritual without reference to Tsembaga conceptions, but it is reasonable to regard the conceptions of a people as part of the mechanism that induces their behavior" (88).

However, if certain authors in the theoretical literature of population regulation are correct, the sentiments of the people involved regarding their own population pressure would scarcely be important, because the potential for population explosion exists everywhere to such a degree that there must always be some mechanism to prevent it. According to the conclusions of Hassan, based upon calculations given at length in a previous article,

" ... the average maximum potential of population growth in primitive groups can be calculated as follows: given an average reproductive span of 18 years, a spacing period of 2.5 years (including allowance for foetal death), 12% sterility, and 10% maternal mortality, 5.7 children per female can be produced. At a rate of 40-50% mortality before adulthood, the number of surviving children per female would be 2.85-3.4, amounting to an annual population growth rate of 1.77-2.65% (doubling time 39-26 years). With a desired spacing period of 3.5 years (equivalent to a net spacing period of 3.3 years with 20% infant mortality) and the same estimates of reproductive span, sterility, maternal mortality, and mortality before adulthood, the number of surviving children per female is 2.16-2.59 and the annual growth rate 0.41.3% (doubling time 180-54 years)" (89).

In view of Hassan's calculation that an average rate of population increase of 0.1% "would allow two persons to populate the whole earth to its present density in only 20,000 years" (90), it is relatively easy to accept his conclusion that:

" ... to maintain a stable population there must have existed a need to eliminate 10-20% of potential infants beyond the reduction warranted to safeguard the health of the female and her offspring by prolonging the spacing period. The total reduction required for both a prolonged spacing period and stabilization of population size amounts to about 25-35% of all potential offspring. The prevalence of birth control practices among primitive groups can thus be easily understood" (91).

The New Guinea Highlands are thought to have been populated for about 10,000 years (92), and there were of course more than two original settlers.

Similarly, Martin has estimated that "at a population growth of 3.4 percent annually, or a doubling every 20 years, 340 years (17 generations) would be the minimum time needed for a band of 100 invaders to saturate the Western hemisphere. Even at a rate of 1.4 percent annually, or a doubling every 50 years, saturation would require only 800 years" (93).

Watson states, regarding the population explosion which he suggests followed the introduction of the sweet potato, that "The Enga ... could have reached their present population of 100,000 in 300 years, from an initial population of 1,146 with an average annual rate of increase of 1.5 percent" (94).

Given this potential for population growth, it seems likely that some kind of control must be in operation in the Highlands, as among all human groups, or the population of the Highlands would far exceed the present three-quarters of a million (95). However, it is not obvious what form the regulation would take or how much influence the regulatory mechanism would have over other aspects of the social structure. If the potential for population explosion is a constant for all human societies, as these calculations suggest, it cannot be used as a *sufficient* condition in explaining the existence of a phenomenon particular to a given culture area, such as aversion toward women in the Highlands.

Several authors have proposed very ambitious explanations for large-scale societal phenomena as forms of population regulation. For example, Divale has attempted to explain female infanticide, polygyny, and warfare, usually over women, as related practices whose main function is to control excess population (96); Divale and Harris (97) have suggested that the "male supremacist complex" in horticultural and band societies provides a framework which supports population control by means of female infanticide, and that warfare "functions to maintain the male supremacist complex and thereby to provide the practical exigencies and ideological imperatives for post-partum cultural selection against female infants" (98).

Siskind has suggested that "an artificially or culturally produced scarcity of women provides a density dependent mechanism that functions to disperse groups of hunting-and-gathering or hunting-and-agricultural populations in accordance with the availability of game, where game is the limiting factor" (99). Women, according to this argument, are "the incentives for hunting and the goal of raiding" (100), and raiding "itself keeps groups at a distance from one another, thus dispersing hunters" (101).

According to Wynne-Edwards, referring to human as well as to animal societies, " ... society is no more and no less than the organization necessary for the staging of conventional competition. At once it assumes a crisp definition: a society is an organization of individuals that is capable of providing conventional competition among its members" (102); furthermore, "the control of population density ... can be effectively provided simply by ... conventional competition" (103).

Finally, Hayden maintains, in an argument too lengthy to be quoted in detail, that the existence of "the incorporation of non-working persons [such as adolescents, the old, and ritual experts] and non-work activities into a group's structure" (104), the sexual division of labor, including a greater workload for women, and male dominance (105) among populations of the present day, as well as the development of the incest taboo, the "elaboration of social roles" and of "kin ... obligations, especially regarding food sharing and required ritual roles" and the "creation of threat by ... magic and harmful supernatural forces" (106) among Australopithecenes, can be explained by the significant contribution of these aspects of social structure to population regulation.

There are many reasons to take issue with these suggestions, one by one; the arguments themselves warrant extensive treatment in another context. There are, however, some general problems relevant to the present discussion. All of these explanatory attempts, like the ones by Glasse and Lindenbaum regarding *horror mulieris* cited at the beginning of the chapter, suffer from trying to explain too much by too little. The underlying theories, which should define the terms in which these explanations are given, are weak for reasons already discussed and for other reasons to be taken up below. Relatively little account has been taken of the numerous other factors which may operate to produce the same societal phenomena, and the particular mechanism by which population levels might be affected has not been detailed.

Some of the constraints which determine population size may be cultural, rather than given in the environment. For example, according to the information presented by Bayliss-Smith, a geographer, five of the six factors which determine the range and magnitude of the subsistence resources available to populations on Pacific atolls are cultural artifacts, such as food preferences (107). We can see from these data that social and cultural factors cannot be explained solely as a function of some set of other pre-existing environmental factors which limit population size, since some of the factors which limit population size may themselves be cultural (108).

An important problem in the underlying theory arises with all of these explanatory suggestions. Rappaport's work on the Maring raises similar questions. Rappaport suggests that Maring ritual serves several ecologically adaptive functions, e.g., regulation of the size of pig herds, of warfare, and of consumption of protein, and redistribution of people and land (109), while the participants in the ritual believe themselves only to be propitiating their ancestors.

Though people may in fact do what is "adaptive" for them, without knowing it, it would be very useful to know how it happens. There are several questions we might ask about the process by which it occurs. First, if we assume that the individual is not conscious of the "adaptive" effects of his activities, we might ask what his precipitating motivation (conscious or unconscious) is, and whether precipitating motivations tend in general to be of a certain type or form. We might also ask whether there is some predictable relationship between the adaptive effect and the form of the precipitating motivation. If the individual is not conscious of the adaptive effect, is there a random relationship between what he is doing and what he thinks he is doing, or does it follow some pattern?

It is also unclear how the perpetuation of the unconsciously adaptive behavior is to be described. For example, we might describe it in behavioristic terms, as an unconscious response to certain stimuli in the environment. Or we might describe it in terms of an unconscious which "knows," in the way that knowledge is ascribed to the unconscious in psychoanalytic theory, or coding ascribed to innate unconscious mental structures by Levi-Strauss and others. Alternatively, we might describe it as a form of natural selection; that is, the behavior selected is no more conscious or volitional than the imitative markings on a Viceroy butterfly (110). The selective pressures would have to be adequately detailed. Given the force of human consciousness in guiding human activities, however, none of these descriptive approaches seems sufficient (111).

These criticisms are not intended to deny that some behavior may have an adaptive effect of which the actor is not conscious. I am attempting rather to suggest some of the serious problems in description and explanation which the notion of unconscious adaptation presents. The resolution of these problems would strengthen explanations given in such terms.

In the particular case of explaining aversion toward women as a form of population regulation, there are some further difficulties, practical rather than theoretical. Although the relative population densities of some Highland groups have been calculated and ranked (112), the degree to which the densities actually represent pressure on resources is difficult to determine, for the many reasons outlined above. The Highland groups for which information has been given about aversion toward women do not intersect precisely with those for whom population density has been calculated. Moreover, it is very difficult to compare among groups the strength of the aversion toward women, because the authorities on the subject have provided information in terms which are not always comparable.

Even leaving aside these caveats, one is not rewarded by making a crude approximation of a correlation between population density and the level of antagonism between the sexes. Population densities for tribes within the Papua New Guinea Highlands are ranked, highest to lowest, by Brown and Podolefsky (113) in the following manner: Chimbu (225 persons/mi^2), Mae Enga, Huli, Mt. Hagen, Gadsup, Siane, Maring, and South Fore (30.8 persons/mi^2). The Chimbu, with the highest population density, are not especially noted for their high level of antagonism, while the men of South Fore, with the lowest population density, are among the most antagonistic and violent of all Highland peoples.

Finally, the prevalence of micro-climate variation within tribal areas as well as between them (114), and the "marked ecological effects" of "small differences in weather" (115), including differences in crop productivity (116), mean that factors which would influence population pressure may differ significantly within a small geographical area. A comparison of groups for *horror mulieris* as a function of population pressure should ideally take these factors, as well as land- and people- redistributive mechanisms, into account. Unfortunately the data do not permit such a comparison at the present time.

It seems that Sweeney was right – and wrong. Looking at society only in terms of natality, reproduction, and mortality *is* boring – but fortunately the "facts" are more interesting than that.

Notes – Chapter Five

1. Lindenbaum 1972:247-248.
2. Sanday 1981:108.
3. Glasse n.d.
4. Bulmer 1971:155.
5. ibid:156.
6. Meggitt 1964:210.
7. ibid:207; and cf. Meigs 1984:39,41,79.
8. R. Berndt 1962:56 and passim.
9. M. Strathern 1972:164.
10. Newman 1965:76-77.
11. Read 1952:14.
12. Watson 1965b:441.
13. Watson 1965a:307.
14. Watson 1967a:298.
15. Bulmer and Bulmer 1964:47.
16. Sorenson 1972:349,358; 1974:72.
17. Brookfield 1961:444; 1968:50; Brookfield and Brown 1978:20. See Feil 1986 for a discussion of these arguments.
18. Brookfield 1964:21-22.
19. ibid:22.
20. Brookfield 1959:136; 1961:439-440.
21. Robbins 1963:54; Brookfield 1964:32.
22. Brookfield and Brown 1963:76.
23. Brookfield 1964:25,31.
24. Brookfield 1961:439.
25. Clarke 1971:157,164.
26. Watson 1965b:447; Brown 1978: 284-285.
27. Howells 1973:173-174; Brookfield and Brown 1963:74; Dornstreich 1974:8; A. Strathern 1971b:133.
28. Venkatachalam 1962:10,76-78; Hipsley and Kirk 1965:79; Clarke 1971:24-25; Rappaport 1984:468.
29. Rappaport 1968:87.
30. ibid:284.
31. Brown and Podolefsky 1976:215.
32. Rappaport 1968:87. However, some New Guineans may have an organic adaptation, perhaps specialized intestinal flora, which allows them to subsist healthily on a protein intake lower than generally presumed necessary (Watson 1977:62-63, quoting Oomen 1970).
33. Kelly 1968:43; Meggitt 1977:14.

Population Regulation

34. Brookfield and Brown 1963:79.
35. Sorenson 1972:358.
36. Reay 1967:4.
37. Clarke 1971:156 and cf. Sillitoe 1977:78 and Mandeville 1979:112.
38. Bulmer 1971:158.
39. Sillitoe 1977:73-74.
40. Brown and Podolefsky 1976:213.
41. Kelly 1968:46.
42. Rappaport 1968:93.
43. Brown 1978:276.
44. Brush 1975:808, quoting Street 1969.
45. Harris 1978:291.
46. ibid:296.
47. Clarke 1971:188, quoting W. Allan 1965:89.
48. Clarke ibid:181.
49. Brush 1975:807-808.
50. ibid.
51. Dewar 1984:605,610.
52. ibid:606.
53. ibid:610.
54. ibid:602.
55. Dewar (ibid:606) observes that the assumption that population levels are equibrial (and that the equibrial level is determined by the productive capacity of the environment) has "never been subjected to a formal test."
56. ibid:609.
57. Wood and Smouse (1982), for example, suggest that population size among the Gainj is regulated in part by density-dependent mortality (but not fertility) affecting some age groups more than others, and that the population as a whole is food-limited in size.
58. Dewar 1984:608,610.
59. Kelly 1968:58.
60. Brookfield and Brown 1963:11.
61. ibid:117.
62. Clarke 1971:187 and see Brush 1975:800-801.
63. Kelly 1968:46.
64. Brookfield and Brown 1963:122. More recently, however, some Chimbu groups are beginning to approach the minimum level of acreage needed per capita (Harris 1978:288).
65. Rappaport 1968:95.
66. ibid:94.
67. Sillitoe 1977:78.
68. Wynne-Edwards 1964:1544.
69. ibid.
70. Hayden 1972:205.
71. Vayda 1969:214.

72. Wynne-Edwards 1964:1545; Siskind 1973:236. Alland and McCay (1973:172), who reject the existence of adaptive mechanisms which maintain the population below carrying capacity, suggest that instead, apparent population stability is due to "a single limiting factor in the environment." But this factor then *is* one (the major one) of the determinants of carrying capacity, and ought to be taken into a recalculation of the actual carrying capacity.
73. Hassan 1981:166 ff.
74. ibid:175.
75. ibid:167.
76. ibid.
77. ibid:164.
78. ibid:170.
79. White 1975.
80. Hassan 1981:158-159. Sober and Lewontin (1984:126) and Sober (1984b:174) suggest that a current adaptation is always the result of the historical process of selection under *previous* conditions, so that the current set of adaptations may be inherently somewhat out of phase with current conditions.
81. Douglas 1966a:266.
82. Clarke 1971:156.
83. ibid:188.
84. ibid.
85. e.g. Divale 1970:178.
86. e.g., Reay 1967:13; Sillitoe 1977:75; Meggitt 1977:183.
87. Siskind 1973:239.
88. Rappaport 1968:6-7. More recently, Rappaport (1984:330) states that "there may be no simple, direct relationship between the amount of testable, empirical knowledge encoded in a people's general understandings of the world and the ecological appropriateness of the behavior elicited by those understandings."
89. Hassan 1973:540.
90. ibid:538.
91. ibid:540.
92. Watson 1967a:82.
93. Martin 1973:970.
94. Watson 1965a:302.
95. Bulmer and Bulmer 1964:39.
96. Divale 1972:224.
97. Divale and Harris 1976.
98. ibid:527.
99. Siskind 1973:226.
100. ibid:232.
101. ibid:236.
102. Wynne-Edwards 1964:1545.
103. ibid.
104. Hayden 1972:212.

105. ibid:213.
106. ibid:215.
107. Bayliss-Smith 1974:284.
108. In a similar vein, Rappaport (1984:435 and cf. ibid:340) argues that the nutritional needs of the Tsembaga Maring could have been better met by a different system of pig husbandry and slaughter, but that the prevailing methods "were central to the maintenance and regulation of social and political relations as well as ecosystemic relations and dietary intake." Here again, societal phenomena are seen not to be rigidly determined by biological constraints, but nearly the reverse: that nutrition and environmental relations are in this case constrained by socio-political considerations.
109. Rappaport 1968:3.
110. Alland and McCay suggest that cultural behavior is "shaped," as in Skinnerian operant conditioning - that is, reinforced or extinguished - by natural selection, and that therefore "cultural adaptation need not be a conscious process" (1973:172). In a later work, however, Alland has a different assessment of the utility of this point of view: "that only a small segment of culture can be explained this way" (1975:70), and that Levi-Straussian or Chomskian mental structures also constrain belief and behavior.
111. Recently, Rappaport (1984:320-324) has suggested that conscious decision making played an important role in Maring ecological, socio-economic, and ritual behavior, but that the ritual cycle "set the terms by which decisions of certain sorts were to be made" (ibid:322).
112. Brown and Podolefsky 1976:214-215; Sillitoe 1977:72-73.
113. Brown and Podolefsky 1976:214-215.
114. Brookfield 1961:440-441.
115. Brookfield 1964:25.
116. Watson 1967a:93.

6

Aversion Toward Women as a Population Regulatory Device, II: Problems in Explanation

I

In the previous chapter, I discussed some of the practical and theoretical problems involved in assessing population pressure in the New Guinea Highlands. Now I would like to pay close attention to the effect, if any, of population pressure on the relationship between men and women. And finally, I will examine some of the problems in the theory of cultural adaptation, on which any explanation in terms of population regulation rests.

Suppose that for the sake of argument we assume that population pressure on scarce resources can be accurately assessed. In that case, we can ask whether aversion toward women would in some way be effective in regulating population size.

The regulation of the reproductive rate in pre-modern societies probably takes place through a combination of physiological and cultural controls. The interaction between the two types of controls and among the various factors which constitute the controls may be quite complex (1). According to Hassan, the length of the reproductive span, the child-spacing period, and survivorship to child-bearing age are "key variables" (2) which affect the net reproduction rate (and hence population size), and they are themselves affected by many biological and socio-cultural factors.

The relative importance of various mechanisms of population size regulation in humans is still a matter of debate (3). In brief, physiological mechanisms of population regulation have been suggested, such as adreno-pituitary and other hormonal effects of the mother on the fetus, and an increase in the malformation rate and in lethal genetic factors with increased maternal stress and poor maternal nutrition (4).

The relationship between body fat in the mother as a measure of the availability of appropriate food and the work necessary to obtain it, prolonged nursing, amenorrhea, and birth spacing has recently received considerable attention (5), as has the relationship between prolonged lactation, the secretion of the hormone prolactin by the mother, and the resulting suppression of ovulation for long periods (6).

In each of these models, socio-economic and cultural factors determine the way in which the physiological means of birth spacing find expression, and in some cases, cultural factors may override the suggested physiological mechanism, making it inoperative.

Factors which are purely cultural or socio-economic, and not mediated by physiological mechanism, may also affect the net reproduction rate. In the New Guinea Highlands, many of these factors are part of the structural relationship between men and women, such as spinsterhood, age of first marriage for women, age of wife at death of husband and number of potential reproductive years remaining, remarriage of widows and divorcees, the extent of premarital and extramarital intercourse, avoidance between bride and groom after marriage, periods of abstinence for ritual or social reasons, extramarital "sexual outlets for males" (7) including homosexuality and rape, and the lower birth rate associated with polygyny (8).

The most important and effective means of population size regulation in the Highlands are abortion (9), and particularly, the post-partum taboo on sexual relations (10), which Bulmer terms "probably the most important single cultural factor directly determining family size and overall fertility" (11). The post-partum taboo, in combination with prolonged nursing, is widespread and apparently effective in societies inhabiting tropical rainy environments worldwide (12).

In using either of these methods, women and men can see the immediate cause and effect relationship of their actions. Aversion toward women as a regulator of population size, on the other hand, is dependent upon an elaborate feedback of conscious and unconscious psychological and cultural phenomena. Other such complexities exist in human society, of course, but it is probable that a simpler form of regulation is more effective.

Apart from the fact that other forms of population regulation are apparently of greater importance, there are also inherent limitations to the effectiveness of *horror mulieris* as a regulatory device. There are several reasons to question the extent to which aversion toward women results in a significant marginal diminution of conception rates.

The most polluting aspect of women's sexuality in the Highlands, associated with the greatest degree of repugnance, is considered to be menstruation and the first few days which follow it. Avoidance during this non-ovulatory time would not diminish the rate of conception. In fact, avoidance during this period of time may have the effect of increasing both the sperm count and the frequency of intercourse during ovulation, and thus increasing the rate of conception (13). Among the Huli, for example, the only days of the menstrual cycle which are not under some prohibition against intercourse coincide with the ovulatory period (14).

Another reason that aversion toward women may not regulate the population size is that it is bachelors and younger men who have the greatest expressed aversion and fear toward women, not older married men (15). As we have seen, younger men are in fact exhorted by older men to fear the pollutive dangers of women and to avoid intercourse, but the older men themselves are much more relaxed in their own behavior about the supposed dangers. Despite the expressed fear of women, older men in most Highland societies have an active interest in sex (16) and in procreation (17). They may actively wish to have children, and in some cases feel that women are deliberately avoiding reproduction.

Because of polygyny and because of other social structural factors which have been outlined in previous chapters, women of child-bearing age are in general married to older men. Avoidance by bachelors and younger men, but not by older men, would thus have little effect on reproductive rates. Moreover, many of the younger married men are married to young adolescent girls apparently affected by adolescent infertility (18), which has been widely reported for Melanesia (19) as well as elsewhere.

In animal and human populations, the number of offspring in the -1 generation (the offspring generation) is dependent upon the number of females in the breeding population of the 0 generation (the parent generation). Aversion toward women would at most remove men, and not women, from the breeding population. A parallel aversion, such as fear or disgust toward the sexuality of men, is virtually unreported for women in the Highlands area. The exceptions seem mainly to concern the effect of the parents' sexual relations upon infants: for example, a fear that semen might find its way into the mother's milk and poison the child (20) or otherwise interfere with nursing (21). This limited concept of pollution on the part of women would mainly encourage adherence to the post-partum taboo.

On the other hand, important forms of population control do indeed seem to be dependent upon the voluntary measures practiced by women, although not for reasons of aversion toward men.

According to Bulmer, the spacing of children in the Highlands, by means including the length of the post-partum taboo, may be a function of "the extent to which women have to undertake demanding domestic and garden activities on a purely individual basis, rather than co-operatively" (22).

Maternal workload, including the nutritional and caloric demands of pregnancy, lactation, and transportation of young children, and including food production and other work, is considered to be a significant determinant of fertility in Pleistocene and present-day hunter-gatherer populations as well (23).

The social structure of the relationship between women and men may also profoundly influence the context in which reproductive decisions are made in the Highlands. Bulmer suggests that "Married women may also attempt abortions if they are dissatisfied with their marriages and the birth and survival of a child would make it more difficult for them to leave their husbands, or to annoy their husbands" (24).

Bowers notes that " ... a girl tries to avoid pregnancy for the first year or two [after marriage], partly to keep up her attractive appearance as long as possible, partly to minimize the possibility of being trapped by children into maintaining a miserable marriage" (25). According to M. Strathern, infanticide may be motivated by anger at the husband (26).

It is obvious that these voluntary measures are themselves influenced by factors stemming from the social structure, including the unequal division of labor by sex, antagonism between husbands and wives, the allocation of power between men and women, and the composition of work groups.

Thus it seems that the desire for birth control may be *due* to antagonism between the sexes, rather than the reverse order of causation suggested by Lindenbaum and the other authors cited at the beginning of the previous chapter. In their argument, antagonism between the sexes appears to be a *result* of the pre-existing need for birth control, and I am suggesting just the opposite: that women in the Highlands may avoid procreation because of their structural role vis à vis men.

It seems almost too obvious to suggest that the structural relationship between men and women has a fundamental effect on the way in which they reproduce, and yet this factor is very often overlooked in anthropological studies.

There is some evidence, however, outside the anthropological literature that the relationship between the sexes affects reproductive decision-making in various ways in other societies. For example, studies in Jamaica, the U.S., Puerto Rico, and elsewhere (27) have suggested that the type of relationship between men and women, including such factors as male dominance, communication between spouses, modesty or reticence on the part of women, and suspicion of infidelity, may affect the way in which women have children or refrain from having them.

In Jamaica, women in informal consensual unions often wish to have children to increase the stability or permanency of the unions (28), and conversely, married women have the highest proportion of continuing contraceptive use (29). In Mexico, women were found to fear using contraception because it might undermine the husband's authority (30). These studies support the idea that the voluntary control of reproduction by women may be determined in part by their structural relationship with men.

Hayden, in the elaborate argument cited in the previous chapter, suggests that population control measures undertaken by women are a function of the unequal division of labor between the sexes. However, he further suggests that the inequality itself is a societal mechanism for encouraging women to limit the number of their offspring (31). Similarly, Stott states that "this unequal division of labor to the disadvantage of women is a cultural provision which has had survival value by the limitation of fertility" (32), but he thinks that the limitation occurs through physiological mechanisms, rather than by voluntary measures.

The suggestions of Hayden and Stott might be criticized on several grounds. The reasons which they give for the unequal division of labor, the way in which the notion of adaptation is employed in their arguments, and the Panglossian tone of the explanation of inequality, assuming that somehow everything is for the best – all of these assumptions are questionable. However, the suggestion that voluntary measures of fertility control may vary according to the amount and type of labor undertaken by women seems a valid one. I have argued in an earlier chapter that the unequal division of labor between the sexes in the New Guinea Highlands may be traced to economic and social structural factors, rather than to ecologically "adaptive" ones.

A final reason that aversion toward women may not regulate population size is that many Highland groups actively recruit new adult members (33), or at the least, admit those who have been routed in warfare from elsewhere or who are cognatically related (34). An argument could be made to the effect that admitting adult, rather than infant, members to the society saves the society the energy of bringing them up. However, adult recruits to a society are less tractable and have more conflictual allegiances than members of a society socialized into it from birth. The recruitment of new adult members is probably due to the need for group defense in a situation of endemic warfare, but it certainly does not suggest that the society is impinging so closely on its resources that the high social and psychological cost of sexual antagonism can be attributed to, or "written off" against, an ineluctable population pressure.

II

A related set of problems concerning the use, in explanation, of ecological variables as the direct cause of relations between the sexes is illustrated by the work of Sanday (35). Sanday, using cross-cultural statistical correlations, has attempted to link male dominance with environmental factors in a number of ways, including the relationships between a) the food supply and the number of sexual pollution beliefs, b) gender origin symbolism and the dominant mode of subsistence, c) male dominance and the type of subsistence economy, d) male dominance, the experience of migration, and the nature of the food supply, and e) male dominance, chronic warfare, and food stress. Her assertion that male dominance is "associated with increasing technological complexity, an animal economy, sexual segregation in work, a symbolic orientation to the male creative principle ..." (36), as well as the positive statistical correlation she finds between chronic warfare and male dominance, and between migration and male dominance, are all supported by the New Guinea Highlands material.

However, Sanday's analysis poses a number of serious theoretical problems, touched upon only briefly here, which make it difficult to accept many of her conclusions. First, although her argument rests upon some description of the techno-environmental subsistence base, which is taken as the independent variable in many of the correlations, there is a fundamental problem with the measures used to represent the environment. At times the subjective impression or "sense" of the people themselves (37) about the environment is used to measure the environment, which is itself represented by "the ease and consistency of [the] quest for survival" (38). However, it seems unlikely that a people's "sense" of the environment is a sophisticated enough measure of complex ecological variables.

At other times, seemingly less subjective measures (or at least descriptions) are used to represent the environment, such as the hunting of large game animals, or a "lush environment, where food is derived from the earth" (39). But here again, these measures do not do justice to the complexities of such important ecological ratios as the calorie expended per calorie returned in various types of subsistence activities, or the relative contribution of various types of food (and their production) to overall caloric and mineral intake, as well as protein intake.

Sanday seems to sidestep these issues by dividing subsistence economies according to whether the predominant mode of acquiring food emphasizes animals or plants (40), but gives no measurable or ostensive correlates to the word "emphasizes." In view of the major caloric and nutritional contribution of vegetable foods to the diet even of hunter-gatherers, a term with less reference (than "emphasizes") to beliefs and psychological states, and with more precise reference to inputs and outputs of matter, time, caloric energy, etc., seems to be called for.

Similarly, Sanday gives the hunting of large game animals a role as a major determinant of belief system, sex-role behavior, and child-rearing practices, but she seems to sidestep the energy ratio issues involved in the relative importance of hunting by using the "psychological energy expended in this effort" (41) as the sole criterion of its importance, "regardless of the contribution of meat to the overall diet" and "whether or not men spend part or most of their time in hunting activities" (42).

The use of terms which are subject to a wide range of interpretation, such as "energy vital to human survival" (43), "inner energy" (44), and "stress" (45) (sometimes used to mean environmental factors and sometimes social or psychological ones (46)), also does not contribute to the overall precision of Sanday's argument.

A second kind of problem in Sanday's analysis, stated briefly, is that ideation (that is, ideas, thoughts, beliefs) is used to explain social and economic structure and sex-role behavior, rather than the reverse. This line of argument runs through the book, in such assertions as that "male dominance results if adversity is blamed on matters having to do with women" (47), that "sex role plans determine the sexual division of labor" (48), that the Hadza's belief "that contact with menstrual blood is dangerous ... is the wedge that drives the sexes apart" (49), and that "the occurrence of menstrual taboos and other intersexual avoidance practices" are to be treated as "a system of meaningful symbols in which the actual relationship between the sexes plays a negligible role" (50).

Problems in Explanation 123

In contrast, my own argument throughout the present analysis of Highland society has been that societal ideas and beliefs themselves, in particular those regarding the relationship between the sexes, can be seen as a function of socio-political and economic forces. Simplicity and prudence would suggest that the "actual relationship between the sexes" (itself constrained by larger forces of social structure and economic organization, and ultimately by relatively fixed techno-environmental constraints) is responsible for *ideas* about the sexes, rather than the reverse.

Because Sanday has in general omitted the effects of economic and socio-political forces in her argument, statistically correlating mostly "ecological" variables with ideational ones, the importance of intervening variables is lost. For example, a fluctuating food supply with "storage techniques to insure against periods of famine" is correlated with a high percentage of societies in which the sexes are unequal (51), as well as with a slightly higher number of sexual pollution beliefs (52), and this Sanday suggests is due to the need for male dominance in the face of "stress" (as evidenced by the potential for famine) (53). But she does not consider the effects of storage, food accumulation, and capital formation, and the subsequent need for its distribution and defense, on the social structure, and the effects in turn of the social structure on the ordering of groups of men, which may lead to male dominance.

Finally, some of Sanday's conclusions, in particular those regarding the New Guinea Highlands, are based on partial or non-contextual statements of fact. For example, she suggests (with regard to a statistical sample of 111 societies) that "people conserve sexual energy in societies where the food supply is uncertain ... curtail[ing] the expenditure of inner energy when outer sources of replenishment are unreliable" (54), citing Lindenbaum's (55) similar argument in support of her position. She then states that "such fears often decline with the introduction of new technology and food sources" (56), but the term "often" is based on a statement by Lindenbaum which apparently refers only to the New Guinea Highlands and is itself unsupported by any specific data (57).

Similarly, a statement by Sanday adduced in support of the "fear of excess fertility" (58), and apparently based on a mistaken example (59), is factually incorrect, namely that "infanticide and the killing of widows within 24 hours after the death of their husbands is common" in the New Guinea Highlands (60).

Sanday's depiction of the relations between men and women of the Fore (on which she bases a more general conclusion about cross-cultural inter-sexual relations) is also rather out of line with their portrayal in the ethnographic literature (61). She describes Fore women as having "considerable autonomy" and "female power" (62), and says that "the Fore exhibit behavior suggestive of mythical male dominance" (63), defined earlier as "the ambiguous ... relationship between the sexes in societies where females have political and economic power, but men act as if males were the dominant sex" (64). There is simply no evidence that Fore women have political and economic power, and therefore the force of her contrast of the Fore with the Enga, among whom "male dominance ... seems very real" (65), is considerably diminished.

As well, the conclusion which she bases upon this contrast is cast into doubt, namely that "real male dominance evolves when the primary dependence for social continuity during times of severe stress is found in the male world, and mythical male dominance evolves when the primary dependence for social continuity involves both males and females" (66).

The questions which trouble the explanatory power of Sanday's statistical correlations - that is, measures of cross-cultural similarities which may not represent the most relevant factors, lack of specificity in the use of terms which should describe environmental inputs and outputs, absence of important intervening variables, especially those pertaining to economic and social structure, and a problematical set of relationships among ecology, economy, socio-political structure, inter-sexual relations, and ideation - are not unique to Sanday's analysis. They would be worth considering with regard to other discussions of the relationship between ecology and social structure, especially with regard to relations between the sexes, as well.

III

The question of whether fear of women is a form of "birth control" provides a good working example of the problems entailed by explanations given in ecological and population regulatory terms. The idea of explaining social phenomena with ultimate reference to ecological and/or economic necessity is a valid one, although many factors of socio-political and economic organization, as well as psychological, conceptual, and ritual organization, may intervene between the "first causes" and the actual observable social phenomena.

But another kind of important issue is a little different than only disentangling the various threads of causality – though that is worthy, and difficult, enough. We ought to ask what kinds of things we need to know in order even to frame the question properly, of the relationship between a conceptual/psychological phenomenon such as aversion toward women on the one hand and the biotic adaptation of a population to its ecological setting on the other. The terms in which to ask and answer these sorts of questions are themselves in need of examination. As a small step in that direction, I would like to take up some of the problems in the theory of cultural adaptation, a crucial notion for explanations given in ecological and population regulatory terms.

The problems involved in the notion of cultural adaptation provide a good example of a crucial concept on which a theory or a hypothesis depends, and the way in which it can undermine the rest of an explanation if it is not very well understood in itself.

Cultural adaptation has very often been treated as though the words "adaptation" and "adaptive" were to be understood in a manner fully analogous to the use of the same terms in Darwinian and post-Darwinian evolutionary theory. I would argue that the analogy is flawed, and that it gives rise to many confusions, which ramify through ecological explanation. In fact the theory of adaptation is problematical even when it deals solely with organic animal adaptation, and the problems are much compounded in its analogical application to human social behavior.

My intention in criticising the notion of adaptation is not to maintain that cultural adaptation does not exist, that it may not be a major determinant of behavior, or that a theory for it is logically impossible. Instead, I believe that examining some of the definitional problems and contradictory or confused aspects of the notion of adaptation may help to strengthen the concept and the use to which it is put in explanation.

The notion of cultural or behavioral adaptation is ostensibly based upon the Darwinian model of adaptation and selection, but the many discrepancies between the two models of adaptation can cause quite a bit of confusion.

The Darwinian model of selection posits the increase over time of the percentage of the population which manifests a given inheritable adaptive characteristic; the adaptive advantage of the characteristic confers differential reproductive success upon the characteristic-bearing individual and its offspring. Selection therefore takes place among individuals, and adaptation may be defined as that which confers positive differential reproductive success.

In the case of a human society's behavioral or cultural adaptation to the environment, however, there are numerous respects in which this model of adaptation cannot be applied without qualification.

The first problem is that the criteria for adaptation are not generally agreed upon. What is to be maximized in the cultural adaptation of a human society? Various suggestions have been or might be made, including the size of the population in numbers, the efficiency of energy capture by the society (67), the health and physical well-being of the individuals in the society, or the quality of life for individuals. It is interesting that the criteria for better or worse adapted populations are not clear for animal populations, either. Such measures as the number of individuals, the current rate of change in numerical size, reduction in number, ecological versatility, the ability to exploit new ecological niches, numerical stability, and total biomass (68) have been suggested.

The criteria of physical well-being and quality of life of the members of a society, although they appear to differ radically from the Darwinian criteria for adaptation, may in fact be intimately, though tacitly, involved in the assessment of adaptiveness. It is probably not the case that

Problems in Explanation

any arrangement of social relations would be considered "adaptive" by most people. There are many borderline cases which are difficult to assess, but the ones which may be easily rejected are those which run violently counter to our notion of what human life should be like. Interestingly, we are likely to be more skeptical of claims regarding the adaptiveness of societies at or near our own level of technological development. For example, if it were held that a society organized as a Fascist dictatorship were "well adapted," most observers would probably question the notion of adaptation being employed. Nevertheless, various forms of brutality are sometimes described as "adaptive" among non-Western peoples, as though they were somehow less a collection of conscious individuals than we are.

If the quality of life is relevant to adaptation, another question arises. Whose criteria are to be used to assess the quality of life? As Douglas points out, "some needs are cultural" (69), that is, defined as needs by the culture. However, some of these cultural needs may compete for scarce resources with needs which we, as observers, would hold essential to the quality of life. Do we allow in our argument that people may be misguided, relative to some independently set standard, in their desires?

Even assuming that the *observer's* criteria for judging the quality of life are to be used, we might ask how the quality of life is to be assessed for an entire society, particularly in those cases in which the "adaptive" trait benefits some members of the society more than others. Perhaps a "greatest good for the greatest number" rule could be invoked, but if so, its use needs to be made explicit.

A second and related problem is that the criteria for adaptive success or failure have not in general been specified. If any ongoing human society is taken to be adapted, then the formulation becomes tautological, that is, true by definition. On the other hand, there do not seem to be clear-cut criteria for distinguishing those human societies which are well adapted from those which are not.

The work of Alland and McCay offers a notable exception to the problems of tautologous formulation. Noting that "adaptation is properly a technical term in selection theory" (70), they give cultural adaptation an operational definition: "the outcome of technological change that increases the carrying capacity of the environment and is measured by population increase" (71). But these criteria for adaptation pose an important theoretical problem: do we really want to say that larger populations are better adapted? Is a crowded nation better adapted than the Bushmen? Would the Bushmen be better adapted if there were more of them, with a larger technological repertoire? On a planet whose ultimate carrying capacity is limited, we might not want to think of human evolution as entailing ever greater numbers.

Interestingly, the problem of tautology haunts adaptation theory in its application to animals, as well (72). Lewontin (73) suggests that if an adaptive characteristic of an animal is seen as a solution to a problem of design, the tautology is broken, because one can predict in advance which individuals are fitter. In the case of human society, though, it is more difficult to use Lewontin's method, because often the "design problem" itself is due to some factor or factors of social or economic organization, which are themselves in need of explanation, unlike the more or less immutable environmental factors which cause the "problems of design" to which Lewontin is referring.

Several other problems in adaptation theory apply to human as well as to animal adaptation. It is difficult to say that a particular trait is the only one which could fulfill the particular adaptive function that it does; there may be "functional equivalents" which serve the same purpose. Consequently, predictive statements about the form of adaptation may be difficult to make (74). Nor is an adaptive trait always a necessary condition for the existence of a species, or even for its well-being (75). On the other hand, a trait may be involved in a variety of functions, yet it would be mistaken to view it as an adaptation for all of these functions (76).

But there are major problems which the discussion of human adaptation does not entirely share with the theory of evolutionary biology. One of the most important issues is that it is not clear how selection takes place for adaptations in society such as behavior, rules, symbolic systems, or other cultural patterning. This is a crucial problem because the classical notion of adaptation depends upon some incorporated notion of selection. In the Darwinian model of adaptation and selection, selection occurs among individuals and among their offspring. The metaphorical application of the concept of adaptation to society breaks down at exactly

Problems in Explanation 129

this point: it is very difficult to specify how selection might take place among societies.

This problem has several aspects. Instead of considering selection to take place among individuals, we might assume that selection for cultural behavior takes place among groups in the Darwinian sense, substituting groups for individuals in the Darwinian formulation (77). This seems to be the use to which the term "adaptation" has been put in much of the anthropological literature.

There are, however, numerous difficulties with a formulation of this kind regarding human societies. The definition of a "group" with a culture must be clearly specified to prevent the formulation from becoming tautologous. It is rather rare that a human group dies out entirely. The survivors may "regroup" with many of the same cultural traits, or they may take these traits elsewhere, even introducing some of them to another group. Limits might be established as to what is to be considered "the same" ongoing group (78), in terms of the continuing percentage of the same socio-cultural traits, or the same members, or their offspring inculcated in a way appropriate to the culture. This is of some importance to the notion of the group as a unit of adaptation, because all groups undergo replacement of their membership over time, as well as some degree of cultural change. In a situation of constant fission and fusion, such as that found in the New Guinea Highlands, the problem of "group" definition is even more difficult.

It is not clear what would constitute adaptive failure for a cultural group, if any remaining aggregate of individuals, or any set of cultural characteristics carried by a group of individuals, can be seen as a continuation of the group in some form.

Another problem is that the number of societies among which selection is assumed to take place is very small in a given region, relative to the number of individuals among whom selection takes place in the Darwinian sense. Hence variability from which selection is made, an important factor in organic evolutionary adaptation, is limited.

In many cases the traits which are said to be adaptive are actually shared by all of the groups in the area (the area as defined by ecological and topographical features). In this latter case it would actually be impossible for selection to take place among the groups for these traits (unless it had taken place in the past and the societies lacking the characteristic were no longer extant).

Still a further complication is that the entire cultural and ecological area has sometimes been, if only implicitly, taken as the unit of adaptation, leading to a somewhat confusing analysis. For example, Meggitt suggests that the practice of eating rotten pork distributed in ceremonial exchange, and the resulting deaths from enteritis, "may operate selectively to restrict, as well as to stimulate, the growth of particular clans" and presents this as negative "feedback" in the total system of adaptation (79). It is difficult to understand what the term "selection" means, as it is used in this argument. The only possible sense in which the restriction of the growth of some subgroups could be adaptive would be if the entire set of intertribal relations were taken as the unit of adaptation (80). But in that case, "adaptation" would not confer any advantage, for advantage implies comparison, and there would be no unit of similar magnitude with which to make a comparison. (The particular clans themselves could not be the units of selection, as the selective advantage to the clan itself of death and of restriction of growth in this situation is rather questionable.)

A further problem in testing an entire society, as opposed to its members, for differential reproductive success is that, given a certain technology, societies presumably cannot expand beyond a certain size, because of the limitations posed by the food supply or other factors. Consequently, the number of individuals in the society cannot be taken *per se* as an indicator of successful adaptation (81).

This problem exists in the analysis of adaptation in animals also (82), in which the mechanism of population size regulation and its relationship to adaptation is a matter of ongoing debate (83).

There appear to be many problems involved in considering human societies as units of adaptation in a manner analogous to the treatment of individuals in Darwinian adaptation theory. On the other hand, it is difficult to treat human societal adaptations as merely a statistical aggregate of the adaptations of individuals (84) (as Williams (85) has suggested for animal societies), although this suggestion has been made by several authors (86). It is difficult and unhelpful to take such human social phenomena as beliefs, norms, expectations, rules, and values and reduce them analytically solely to the adaptive actions of individuals, especially because these phenomena are the result of the *interactions* of individuals (87). Moreover, as Rappaport points out, cultural conventions typically constrain, rather than abet, individual competition, either against one another or vis à vis the environment (88).

The problem of individual versus group selection, and such variants as the selection of an individual's genes through its kin, has been extensively debated in studies of animal populations as well (89). The attempt by sociobiologists to reduce the explanation of human social behavior to a matter of genetic inheritance has been disputed on numerous grounds (90). Even the theory regarding the very mechanism of genetic inheritance (apart from its effect on behavior) employed by sociobiology has been criticised as outdated and simplistic (91).

Leaving aside the issues associated with sociobiology, there are several further important problems inherent in using an implicit Darwinian model of adaptation to discuss human societal adaptation. Although cultural traits appear to be the analogical equivalent of genetic traits in such a formulation, the analogy does not carry through very well.

The mechanism by which cultural traits are perpetuated over time differs considerably from the mechanism of Darwinian selection and genetic inheritance. Obviously culture does not need to be inherited genetically, because it can be learned, and transferred from one individual or group to another. Whatever adaptive advantage is conferred by the behavior is also transferred along with the behavior. Most cultural behavior is of course too complex to be inherited as a set instinctual pattern of reaction, and is activated in situations too subtle and complex to be initiated by an innate releasing mechanism, as is supposed for some animal behavior.

Cultural traits can be learned, diffused, altered, or incorporated, retaining the same form but with different functions or meaning, into other social systems. Selection as it is thought of in Darwinian terms does not sufficiently account for these means by which cultural traits may persist. Certainly the advantage cultural traits may bring cannot be measured entirely by reproductive success, as in the Darwinian formulation, so selection cannot account for the statistical aggregate of a trait's continuance, as with genetic traits.

In fact, not every cultural trait is explainable with reference to adaptation and selection. Adaptiveness may have nothing to do with the perpetuation of many cultural traits, because there may be no particular selective pressure constraining a trait to be one way or another. Lewontin and Gould have shown that some traits in biological evolution are not due to adaptation and selection, either (92).

Finally, the time frame in which cultural characteristics are transferred and perpetuated is also considerably different than in organic evolution. New traits may be invented, adopted, or diffused in a matter of a few weeks, not through generations of reproduction as with organic adaptation. If, for example, all of the societies in an area adopt a characteristic more or less at once, selection cannot operate in the usual Darwinian sense.

The time frame in which human socio-cultural adaptation takes place differs from the time frame in the classic form of Darwinian evolution in another significant respect as well. Evolutionary adaptation in the Darwinian sense is blind to the future; that is, adaptations cannot anticipate future selective forces, but are a response to past or present ones. In contrast, some socio-cultural adaptations may be undertaken for the very purpose of influencing future outcomes.

Another set of problems concerns the potential conflict between what is adaptive for the individual and what is adaptive for the society. It is not clear how to discuss the conflict in terms of adaptation and selection. For example, Olson (93) has shown that, in terms of economic rationality, the most rational course of action for the individual in a collectivity is not to make any effort which benefits the collectivity, but to accept his share of the benefits, or "public good," which the collectivity confers more or less equally to all members, thus maximizing the ratio of return to expenditure of effort or goods (94).

Individual advantage and societal advantage cannot always be contrasted in as clear-cut a manner as it may appear, however. Depending on the definition of "individual advantage," the two may not always be entirely separable. Rappaport points out that self-interest for individuals is often *defined* in culturally determined terms, such as honor,

Problems in Explanation

valor, and righteousness, which may conflict with the material advantage of the phenotype or genotype (95).

A second kind of complication is that it is not always clear whether an individual's self-interest is better served by his (or her) contribution to his group, or by more self-centered behavior, or even what "better served" may mean. For example, suppose that members of a minority religious or ethnic group may disaffiliate themselves and become members of the majority. It is likely that material, social, and psychological satisfactions may ensue. But what if, given their previous enculturation, the only way they can continue to "be themselves" - certainly among the most profound forms of human self-interest - is to ensure the persistence of their original group, and hence to give up many of the other advantages? (96). Here again the meaning of "self-interest" is not obvious.

A distinction can also be drawn between what is adaptive in the short run for an individual, and what may be adaptive in the long run for the same individual, especially since these may conflict. This problem is made more difficult by the fact that people are sometimes capable of changing society and their roles in it. For example, we might ask which is more adaptive for a slave, compliance in the short run or organizing a slave revolt in the long run.

A parallel distinction can be drawn between homeostatic adaptation and evolutionary adaption (97). Some traits may be thought of as adaptive relative to the maintenance of homeostasis, or to the "status quo" in the society, and others may be thought of as adaptive relative to change which is beneficial in some way.

Rappaport (98) suggests that the distinction between the maintenance of homeostasis (as it is usually thought of) and the transformation of characteristics (usually thought of as change) in living systems has been overdrawn, and that the transformations themselves are made in order to maintain other crucial variables of the system within viable ranges, and hence in homeostasis as he defines it. Although his suggestion is very useful for the long-run analysis of evolutionary change, I believe that it is worthwhile to keep the distinction between change and stasis for the short-run analysis of human society, in which fundamental changes in the socio-economic order are possible, involving a much greater (and faster) degree of systemic reorganization than the incremental changes of organic evolution.

In the case of humans, the maintenance of the status quo can conflict with change, both for individuals and for societies. Moreover, many behaviors which maintain the homeostasis of the society are not adaptive for the individual, if the individual does not benefit from the status quo. For example, Reay takes the Gluckmanesque position that ritual conflict between men and women among the Kuma of the New Guinea Highlands "must have demonstrated the futility of women's protests ... a protest that failed could not but bolster the established order" (99), and that ritual conflict functioned, along with another ritual, to "renew the unity of the system" (100).

It is important to note that all of these kinds of behavior, namely, homeostatic, evolutionary, those which are beneficial to the individual and not to the society, those which are beneficial to the society or some segment of the society and not to the individual, and those beneficial in the short run but not in the long run and vice versa, have been explained as adaptive, although some of them may be in conflict with others, in practical or logical terms. Criteria are needed for applying one kind of explanation rather than another; until there are such criteria, nearly anything can probably be seen as adaptive in some sense or other.

Rappaport's insightful analysis of the structure of adaptive processes (101) offers a way to assess the adaptiveness of some aspects of organization in society versus others. In brief, he suggests that orderly adaptive processes (102) are necessary for adaptive homeostasis to be maintained in a living system, and that these processes are structured in certain ways which have "substantive implications" (103), that is, implications for the way in which the living system continues to function. He details a set of cybernetic loops in a system, the larger loops of which include the smaller, and a set of hierarchical relations among these subsystems and their regulators, which differ in such dimensions as "specificity [of goals], concreteness, reversibility, arbitrariness, response time, duration, value, sanctity, and authority" (104).

He then defines maladaptation as anomaly in the hierarchical and self-regulatory features which allow homeostatic response (105). Examples of maladaption

Problems in Explanation

include the over-segregation, excessive response, or over-centralization of some subsystems relative to others (106), and particularly, the usurpation by a special-purpose subsystem of the goals or needs of the larger general system of which it is a part (107). Thus Rappaport would probably say that what is adaptive for the society should take precedence in our analysis over what is good for an individual or a subgroup of the society.

But in the case of analyzing human society, some odd problems arise. It is difficult to know what is most adaptive for a whole society (108). Is it a statistical average of everyone's good? What if something benefits some more than others - whose benefit is more important in our analysis? What is to be done about something which is good for the society as a whole, but not necessarily for any of its members (such as being limited by the state to having only one child, as in present-day China)?

Odder still for the purpose of analysis, it is sometimes the case that the operation of the entire society as a system is dependent in the short or medium run on what is beneficial to special interest subgroups and to their continuing successful operation, even though these subgroups have come to dominate the system. For example, in the New Guinea Highlands, the entire social and economic organization of the society is dependent on the successful continuation of ceremonial exchange, *even though* ceremonial exchange in the short run clearly benefits one segment of the society, that is, older men, and serves their "special purpose interests" to a much greater degree than it does anyone else's. Problems like these need to be made explicit to help clarify the notion of what is "adaptive."

In the course of his discussion, Rappaport runs into many of the same issues I have been addressing, although they are not always stated in the same way. Although I am in fundamental agreement with Rappaport, I am bringing out several of the underlying issues in his analysis to show that these problems are implicit in any discussion of the nature of human societal adaptation.

In particular, it seems difficult to use his formulation to establish criteria for judging the adaptiveness of particular traits of behavior or belief, or of forms of social or economic organization, unless they are obviously maladaptive for the self-regulatory hierarchy described above. It seems to be easier to determine what is maladaptive than what is adaptive, according to these terms.

He proposes that the goal of living systems is "simply survival" (109), and that adaptiveness is "identified with the maintenance of a general homeostasis" (110). Adaptive processes are those which "keep the states of crucial variables ... within the ranges of viability" (111). Later, he says that he reserves the term "survival" "for reference to biological (and ecological) continuity" (112), and that "the adaptiveness of aspects of culture may ultimately be assessed in terms of their effects upon the biological components of the systems in which they occur" (113).

These definitions, though reasonable in themselves, seem to lead to an overly general set of criteria for adaptiveness. If biological survival and the maintenance of viable homeostasis (plus perhaps conformity to orderly adaptive structural processes, whose purpose is the maintenance of homeostasis) are the criteria for judging what is adaptive, nearly everything might be seen as adaptive, unless it leads to catastrophe, or causes the system to die out completely. Yet Rappaport himself notes that instances of extinction in human systems are rare (114).

To say that a system goes on surviving does not tell us much about the form in which it survives. I suggest that because we have, at least minimally, certain normative notions about human existence and what it is or ought to be, that the biological continuance per se of a society (or part of a society) is not a sufficient criterion for the adaptiveness of traits in the society.

Another issue implicit in Rappaport's analysis seems to concern the locus or unit of adaptation. In Darwinian theory, adaptation occurs because selection takes place among phenotypic individuals for their genetically transmitted traits. It is not quite clear what Rappaport intends as the analogical equivalent in the analysis of adaptation in systems. He suggests that "survival ... is to be understood as the persistence of processes rather than of entities ... " (115), and that "that which persists is not necessarily any particular feature or component of the adapting system, but simply an organized set of adaptive processes" (116), which suggests that the system itself is the unit of adaptation.

Yet processes do not exist in the abstract, and it is unclear exactly what he means the locus to be, through which adaptation (mediated by selection) occurs, or in fact the role which selection is to play in this analysis of adaptation. Possibly because he subsumes evolutionary change as a kind of homeostatic maintenance or self-regulatory contribution to persistence (117), he does not expand upon the mechanism (by selection or other means) by which traits may be perpetuated. It would be useful here to remember the distinction between "adaptive processes," such as those outlined by Rappaport, and the more usual use of "adaptation" (through selective pressure and reproductive maximization) - Rappaport himself undoubtedly does not mean them to be synonymous.

Rappaport does suggest in a recent work that group selection in human populations may occur, for traits which enhance the persistence of the group (even if they are disadvantageous to the group's constituent members as individuals) (118). But because he *defines* groups as adaptive units (or at least as units in which adaptive processes occur) on the basis of their regulatory response in "unitary" (119) fashion to perturbations, it may be difficult to decide where the boundaries of a "group" as an adaptive unit should be set, and hence at what level adaptive processes and/or adaptation through selection may be taking place.

Overall, however, Rappaport's discussion sheds a good deal of light on the systemic functioning of human society.

The idea that "ideological birth control" regulates population size in the New Guinea Highlands exemplifies many of the theoretical problems which have been the subject of the present discussion.

If the regulation of population size is seen as a form of adaptation to environmental constraints (and there hardly seems to be an alternative reason for population size to be limited), then we must ask in what sense it is an "adaptation," how it is selected for, what the unit of selection is, and how the behavior which constitutes the regulation is perpetuated.

Yet here we are led into a thicket of problems. If on the one hand we try to look at the regulation of population size as the result of an aggregate of individual adaptations - that is, taking the individual as the unit of selection - we run into some of the difficulties already mentioned: a) that the behavior which is assumed to regulate fertility is learned, not innate, so that genetic inheritance is not likely to account for its perpetuation; b) that greater numbers of offspring may be desirable to individuals although they create scarcity in the society as a whole; c) that the individual cannot get feedback about the effects of his or her fertility on environmental variables, and adjust his or her decisions accordingly; and d) that individuals do not invent, one by one, the cultural notions which govern their behavior.

Further, as Alland and McCay (120) point out, "selection – the adaptive process – requires [the] maximization of mean reproductive success ... and here we have a case of minimization of reproductive success." It is difficult to see how a reduction in fertility can be selected for in *individuals*, even in a purely physiological sense – let alone through behavior induced by ideas (121).

On the other hand, if we take the regulation of population size to be an adaptation (and if we adhere to the Darwinian criteria for adaptation) of the society as a whole, then we are left with all of the problems associated with group selection, how selection can take place among societies or groups, what the criteria for adaptiveness among societies should be, and so forth.

We are also left with the problem of where cultural notions come from to begin with, of the sort which would turn out to be "adaptive" – what makes them gain credence and acceptance, what reinforces them, what perpetuates them?

And finally, we are left with the question of how people can adjust their behavior for a set of consciously stated reasons, in order to do something which is of benefit (or "adaptive") for themselves mainly because it is of benefit (or "adaptive") for the society of which they are a part, without actually being conscious of its "adaptive" effect.

These intertwined difficulties are clearly not unique to the New Guinea Highlands situation. Alland and McCay themselves, who follow Williams (122) in rejecting the notion of group adaptation (123), are nonetheless led to the conclusion that, when raising the carrying capacity and migration are impossible, "forms of population control may evolve to produce a stable system ... as well as social practices that indirectly affect fertility levels" (124).

But these social practices cannot be individual adaptations, and so it is likely that they are group adaptations, as difficult as that notion is to provide with ostensible measurements.

This is not to say that the relationship between the sexes ought to be viewed as a kind of direct group adaptation for the purpose of regulating population size. The relationship between the sexes in a society, as I have tried to show throughout the present study, has its proximate causes, and even most of its distal causes, in the society's economic, social structural, and political organization. These forms of organization may ultimately be constrained by techno-environmental factors, including the relationship between resources and population size. Nonetheless, the causal chain which links the techno-environmental with psychological, ideational, behavioral, and structural aspects of the relationship between the sexes is too long and too complex to support an explanation of these aspects as a simple function of techno-environmental determinants.

One final problem concerning adaptation sometimes shows up in the anthropological literature. There is something questionable about some of the uses to which the concept of adaptation is put. For example, Vayda says that "wherever warfare exists it is likely to have been useful or adaptive ... at some time in the course of its development" (125). Similarly, Divale maintains that " ... warfare plays a positive and beneficial role in primitive society" (126). Hayden makes the same sort of statement, asserting that the unequal division of labor between women and men in tropical and sub-tropical climates (the much greater work load falling to women) is "functional" (127).

Adaptation, in these arguments, is like history: it is always seen from the point of view of the survivors. However, warfare is not "adaptive" in any sense of the term for those who are killed in it, and the reasons for excluding them from the unit whose adaptation is under discussion are not clear (128). Similarly, to ignore what is quite maladaptive for at least half the population, that is, women, in the name of overall societal adaptation, is to assign more importance to the well-being of certain segments of the population than to the well-being of others.

We need to be very careful not to use unwittingly our own ethnocentrically biased criteria - which may tacitly take into consideration such factors as age, sex, social class, metropolitan-periphery affiliation, productive ability, state of physical health, and so forth - to weight the well-being of some segments of the population more than others in the assessment of what is "adaptive" for a society.

We have been dealing with the suggestion that men fear and avoid women in the New Guinea Highlands as a form of "ideological birth control." In order to assess the validity of this hypothesis, we have gone all the way back to a discussion of what constitutes "adaptiveness" for cultural phenomena. Sometimes it is necessary to take apart the theory which underlies an explanation, in order to strengthen the theory and question the explanation.

Notes - Chapter Six

1. see Hassan 1980:308 for an indication of the factors involved.
2. ibid.
3. a review and discussion can be found in Cohen 1980 and Lee 1980.
4. Stott 1969, originally 1962.
5. Cohen 1980.
6. Lee 1980.
7. Bulmer 1971:138-150.
8. Bowers 1971:27.
9. Meggitt 1965a:145; M. Strathern 1972:43-44; Bowers 1971:29.
10. e.g., Bulmer 1971:145; M. Strathern 1972:168; Biersack 1984:121.
11. Bulmer 1971:145. In the Highlands of West Irian, the postpartum taboo may be four to six years (Koch 1968a:90; Heider 1970:74), one of the longest reported for any human population.
12. Whiting 1969.
13. Prolonged abstinence may decrease the motility of sperm in the first subsequent ejaculate, however.
14. Glasse 1968:59.
15. Berndt 1962:76; Langness 1967b:1972; Meggitt 1964:210 ff; Read 1952:120.
16. Berndt 1962:188; Reay 1959a:162.
17. Langness 1967:175; Read 1954b:864-868.
18. Lindenbaum notes that " ... in the New Guinea Highlands, ... the onset of menstruation, at eighteen years, is later than in any other population reported to date" (1979:44). Gillison (1980:159) also reports that menarche occurs among the Gimi at 18-19 years of age.

19. Bulmer 1971:142; Chowning 1969.
20. Bulmer 1971:146; M. Strathern 1972:168; Faithorn 1975:137.
21. Meigs 1978:305.
22. Bulmer 1971:147.
23. Hassan 1980; Lee 1980.
24. Bulmer ibid:153.
25. Bowers 1971:27.
26. M. Strathern 1972:44.
27. Back and Hass 1973.
28. Gelber n.d.
29. Powell et al 1978. In modern or modernizing societies, age, socio-economic status, and education must be factored out of such a conclusion. That is, married women in Jamaica also tend overall to be older and of higher socio-economic status, and some of their increased contraceptive use might be due to these factors, rather than to their married state per se.
30. Shedlin 1981:289.
31. Hayden 1972:213-215.
32. Stott 1969:150.
33. A. Strathern 1972:213-215,220-221.
34. Barnes 1962; Watson 1970.
35. Sanday 1981.
36. ibid:171. The fifth association, "stress," is questionable for reasons to be taken up below.
37. ibid:7,68,72,103,185.
38. ibid:65.
39. ibid:68.
40. ibid:69.
41. ibid:65-66.
42. ibid:65.
43. ibid:108.
44. ibid.
45. ibid:171,173,187-188,199,210. Sanday uses migration, "consistency" of food supply, and warfare as indicators of "stress" (ibid:173-174), but since she does not detail the actual mechanism by which these factors affect the economic and social structure, it is unclear just what "stress" is or how it works. In fact, the term "stress" has an elusive meaning in other fields, such as physiology, as well.
46. ibid:181,210.
47. ibid:11.
48. ibid:7.
49. ibid:93.
50. ibid:91.
51. ibid:173.
52. ibid:109.

53. ibid:171-172. It is not clear, however, that the existence of storage techniques is an appropriate indicator for potential famine - in fact it may be the opposite.
54. ibid:108.
55. Lindenbaum 1972.
56. Sanday 1981:108.
57. ibid:265, note 59, regarding Lindenbaum 1972:248.
58. ibid:195.
59. ibid:271, note 28, citing Lindenbaum 1972:248. In fact, Lindenbaum's reference is to the Kaulong and Sengseng of New Britain, not to the peoples of the New Guinea Highlands.
60. ibid:195.
61. Berndt 1962; Lindenbaum 1976.
62. Sanday 1981:181.
63. ibid:198.
64. ibid:8.
65. ibid:198.
66. ibid:199.
67. Rappaport (1978a:70) indicates that modern societies are much *less* efficient in the return of energy (in the form of food) to input of energy than hunter-gatherers and slash-and-burn agriculturalists are.
68. Williams 1966:104-106; Sober 1984b:187.
69. Douglas 1966a:267. Similarly, Rappaport (1984:405) questions the correspondence between a people's culturally determined "wants" and the "actual material requirements of the local population, the ecosystem, or the regional population."
70. Alland and McCay 1973:148.
71. ibid:167.
72. e.g., M. Williams 1984:83; Lewontin 1984:239-240,246; Sober 1984b:84; Brandon 1984a:64-66,77-78.
73. Lewontin 1978:215,222; 1984:243,246. A similar point of view is taken by Brandon (1984a:78-79) and Sober (1984b:208).
74. see Hempel 1965:323. Rappaport (1984:353), countering this point of view, argues that "such functional indispensability is at least empirically difficult and probably logically impossible to demonstrate," and that the lack of uniqueness of a given adaptive formulation should not invalidate its usefulness (ibid:439).
75. Lewontin 1978:218.
76. Lewontin 1984:242.
77. Some of the problems concerning group selection in animals are compounded in their application to human societies. For example, the criterion of "propagules" (Brandon 1984b:136; Sober 1984a:192,202, and against this position ibid:203) - that is, offspring groups numerically distinct from the "parent" group - as a measure of reproductive success and hence of adaptation, seems especially inapplicable to human societies. On the other hand, the

Problems in Explanation 143

possibility (Brandon 1984b:134-137; 1985:91; Sober and Lewontin 1984:120; Sober 1984a:192-197,200) of distinguishing between a) selective processes which act at the group level per se, as a result of factors in the group's structure or functioning and b) those selective processes which affect the the group's members as individuals (irrespective of their group membership) but which, when the individuals' adaptive outcomes are added together, have an effect on the adaptive outcome of the group as a whole, does seem applicable to human societies, but very difficult.

78. Looking at the corollary problem, how to know when an animal population or species *ceases* to exist, Slobodkin and Rapoport suggest that extinction occurs either "when there no longer exist any descendants of a population" or when the descendants have changed so much that they have evolved into a new species (cited in R. Rappaport 1978b:80). Unfortunately these criteria help by analogy only a little with the problems outlined here, since we are dealing not with defined species but with fluid human societies, and because extinction is a more clear-cut phenomenon than continuity.

79. Meggitt 1974:199.

80. Peoples objects to Rappaport's implicit use of the entire Maring regional population as the unit of adaptation because it is too large (1982:293), because its constituent groups have conflicting interests (ibid:294), and because it is not an "organized social entity" (ibid.). Rappaport (1982:304) disagrees, characterizing the regional population in this way: "as the loc[us] of the conventions governing the interactions of those subordinate to [it], [it] is [it]self organized," and "an organized whole ... as such can be regarded as [a] proper beneficiar[y] of adaptive processes" (ibid.). Rappaport goes on to describe adaptive processes as homeostatic ones (ibid.): the response "in unitary fashion, to perturbations of either internal or external origin, and, *ipso facto*, ... adaptive." Their disagreement appears to center on the intended meaning of "adaptive": Rappaport refers to homeostatic processes, and Peoples to evolutionary, selective processes.

81. The problems associated with the alternative suggestion of Alland and McCay (1975) are discussed earlier in the chapter.

82. Lewontin 1984:238; Sober 1984b:187,195,198.

83. e.g. Berryman 1981:Chapter 3; Murray 1979: Chapter 3; Williams 1966:29.

84. These individual adaptations could be looked at either as genetically transmitted, or as learned behavior which confers some reproductive or other advantage on an individual.

85. Williams 1966:211,237.

86. see Vayda and McCay 1975 and Orlove 1980 for a discussion and review of these arguments. Countering this point of view, Rappaport (1984:398-399) notes that such analyses, outside sociobiology and ecology, have not been undertaken, and he also

suggests that "the subordination of the properties of groups to the interest of individuals is unwarranted by observation" (ibid:401).

87. Peoples, who describes himself as "one who champions individual advantage" (1982b:307) (i.e., the notion that individuals maximize, in an economically "rational" manner, their individual interests) as a model of explanation for social behaviors, is nonetheless led to abandon this model in explaining Maring ritual and prestation ceremonial, because of the "public good" problem set forth by Olson (see text of Chapter Six in the present study). That is, as Peoples puts it, he cannot maintain that "calculations of personal advantage are sufficient to induce individuals to contribute to the persistence of their groups" (ibid:298).

In fact, Peoples concludes by espousing "natural selection," at the group level, for the cooperative behavior of the group's members. In his view, "warfare acts like natural selection" (ibid: 299) to select out groups without enough reciprocators.

One of the conceptual problems with using warfare as a form of "natural selection" (or even as a selection pressure) is that warfare is not a given in the environment, but is itself an artifact of the same socio-political organization which makes alliance and reciprocity necessary. Thus in People's argument, warfare is both the cause of the entire ritual and ceremonial system, which exists to attract and keep allies, and the "counter[]...force" (ibid:299) (through natural selection) against selfish behavior, which obliges individuals to conform to the system.

It is interesting that Peoples, who begins by rejecting the "neo-functionalism" of Rappaport and others on the grounds that it is "defective ... because it cannot adequately explain why and how individuals adopt behaviors that benefit the group" (ibid:291), concludes by stating that "natural selection can result in the fixation of group-advantageous functional behaviors" (ibid:300) - a conclusion with which most "neo-functionalists" would probably agree.

88. Rappaport 1984:400.

89. Wilson (1975:Chapter 5) reviews these arguments, and they are continued in Brandon and Burian,eds:1984 and Sober,ed:1984.

90. e.g. Montagu et al, 1980; Medawar 1981.

91. King 1980.

92. Lewontin 1978:225,228; 1984:250; Gould and Lewontin 1984:261-266. Some of the interesting issues raised by Lewontin and by Gould suggest analogous questions which might be asked in the study of human societal or cultural "adaptation," especially regarding the delimitation of an adaptive trait. As Lewontin says (1984:241), "if the leg is a trait [in need of explanation as an adaptation], is each part of the leg also a trait?" Similarly, Gould and Lewontin (1984:262) point out that some traits are not in themselves adaptations, but that their form is "a correlated

Problems in Explanation 145

consequence of selection directed elsewhere." Again, some traits may represent not adaptations in themselves, but "the fruitful use of available parts" (ibid:255).

93. Olson 1965. Interestingly, Sober (1984b:184-185,191-192) makes a similar argument regarding the selection of *genetically* inherited traits.

94. Peoples' (1982) analysis of Maring ceremonial in these terms is discussed above. This form of cost/benefit analysis for individuals has been criticized on the grounds that it represents the misapplication of an ethnocentric, bourgeois view of the individual onto a society with a different conception of the individual (Modjeska 1982a:302-303), and that it "reduces incommensurables to the specious simplicity of single metrics ... and in doing so it misrepresents the nature of the world," doing an injustice to the complexity of human thought processes as well (Rappaport 1982:305). Although these criticisms are quite valid, the notion that individual advantage may in some instances be inherently oppposed to societal advantange (which Olson, as well as Peoples, highlights) seems well worth saving - especially because it throws into relief the contrast between the use of the term "adaptation" in the Darwinian sense (in which individual advantage is part of the mechanism of selection) and the problematical use of the term when applied to social groupings *composed* of individuals.

95. Rappaport 1984:400.

96. cf. Vayda and McCay (1975:301) for a contrasting point of view.

97. Alland and McCay (1973:144) and Alland (1975:59) make this distinction clear with respect to organic evolution as well.

98. Rappaport 1979:147; 1978:49-50; 1984:412-413.

99. Reay 1959b:296.

100. ibid:292.

101. Rappaport 1979; 1978a; 1978b.

102. Rappaport 1979:151,160; 1978a:64.

103. Rappaport 1978a:64.

104. Rappaport 1979:156.

105. ibid:161.

106. Rappaport 1978a:59-61.

107. ibid:61; Rappaport 1979:164.

108. Alland suggests that "the direct relationship between population growth and adaptive change occurs only so long as the distribution ... of goods ... is relatively equal" (Alland and McCay 1973:173), but that with the development of stratified societies "other factors intervene to produce culture change" (ibid.), and that demographic success cannot be used in a simple manner as a measure of adaptation in stratified societies (Alland 1975:59-60).

These suggestions are very interesting, but problematical. Following Alland's own criteria for adaptation (referred to earlier in the text of the present work), the absence of demographic success as a criterion for adaptation would make it impossible to speak in Alland's terms about the adaptiveness of traits in most of human society, that is, beyond the stage of egalitarian distribution. Moreover, even in societies as comparatively unstratified as those of the New Guinea Highlands, there are inequalities of distribution – most notably between men and women – which may pose similar problems in assessing the adaptation of the society as a whole.

109. Rappaport 1978a:63.
110. ibid:64.
111. ibid:49.
112. Rappaport 1978b:82.
113. Rappaport 1978a:63-64.
114. Rappaport 1978b:82.
115. ibid:81.
116. Rappaport 1979:149.
117. Rappaport 1984:415.
118. ibid:401.
119. ibid. and cf. ibid:373-374. Hull (1984:143,153), citing Eldredge and Gould and unnamed "group selectionists," also suggests that populations and species, as objects of natural selection, can be seen not as groups composed of individuals but as individuals themselves, "unified and cohesive" homeostatic systems. The theory underlying the notion that selection may occur simultaneously at more than one level – at the level of the individual and the population and/or the gene – is supported by Brandon 1984b:137; Sober 1984a:200; and M. Williams 1984:95.
120. Alland and McCay 1973:155.
121. Unless, as Alland and McCay suggest (ibid:156), an empirical demonstration could be made that a decrease in the total number of offspring gave the existing offspring a better chance of survival.
122. Williams 1966.
123. Alland and McCay 1973:152ff.
124. ibid: 173.
125. Vayda 1969:204.
126. Divale 1970:174.
127. Hayden 1972:213.
128. Hallpike (1977:231), with regard to the Tauade, a non-Highlands group in the Papuan Mountains, distinguishes between different levels of social groupings for which warfare might or might not be called adaptive. He seems to conclude that, given the existence of intertribal warfare, each local group would find fighting "adaptive." But the total intertribal "system" of warfare in his view is not adaptive (and not needed to reduce population pressure). Yet he seems to treat the intertribal pattern of warfare as an outcome, rather than as a determinant, of acts of warfare by local groups. In this case, an argument could be made that intertribal relations, as a "system," are not the relevant unit of analysis to

Problems in Explanation 147

begin with, since they are not a determinant, but an effect, of warlike behavior. Once again, we are faced with the difficult question of where causal determinants and feedback mechanisms should be placed in a scheme of societal and intersocietal "systems" (if they are indeed systems).

7

Conclusion

I

Explaining the character of the relationship between men and women in the New Guinea Highlands has turned out to be a lengthy, and unfinished, job. But in the process, we have seen that the relationship between the sexes must be looked at in the context of nearly all of the environmental, economic, socio-political, psychological, and ideational systems and subsystems of Highland society. The interwoven strands of these forms of organization constitute a network from which it is difficult to extricate a single relationship, but the effort, at least, forces us to begin to disentangle the network itself.

Why is the relationship between the sexes in the New Guinea Highlands the way it is? Why is it so imbued with hostility and suspicion, brutality and drama? What gives rise to the sentiments and attitudes toward women? In terms of what factors or combinations of factors can these things be explained? And how can we assess the various sorts of explanations made about the phenomenon, and by extension, certain types of anthropological explanation in their wider application?

These questions have been the guideposts of my inquiry. In the process of looking for answers, several major avenues of analysis have emerged.

II

The relationship between beliefs and socio-economic structure has been a central and recurrent question. Where do ideas and attitudes about women come from? How are they related to the socio-economic order of Highland society? Although I have been concerned primarily with the relationship between men and women in the Highlands, the methods of analysis I have used in addressing these problems can be applied to other societies as well, including our own.

In the analysis of Highland society, we have seen that it is important not to take ideology at face value. Although the Highlanders are usually reported to hold a certain set of beliefs about women, we have seen that the relationship between ideology and other aspects of Highland society is far from straightforward.

In the Highlands, there is a discrepancy between the reality of social and economic processes and an idealized (or "ideologized") version of what is taking place. Men represent themselves as a corporate group of agnates, members of a men's house which excludes women. In fact, because of the shifting composition of personnel and alliance, they are not a corporate group, or act as one only for transitory periods, and they have many structural stresses and divisive strains among themselves. They are not in fact all agnatic relatives, although patrilineal ideology, shallow genealogical reckoning, and fictive agnation help make it seem so.

Women, according to the "official" set of beliefs, are considered unimportant and of negligible worth, but in fact their role in economic production is crucial to nearly every activity of men, from the most basic activity, such as eating, to the most highly valued symbolic activity, competition for prestige. As well, the role of women in reproduction is obviously necessary for the ongoing existence of the society. Women are thought of as dangerous, but it is life which is dangerous, in an area with continual feuding and warfare. Women are considered divisive, although they are crucial links for affinal inter-group alliance.

The discrepancy between real processes and an idealized version of them is sometimes obscured by more ideology.

Conclusion

There can also be an ambiguity between the two, and the ideology itself can be manipulated – for example, the manipulation by big men of the ambiguity of fictive agnation.

In trying to sort out these relationships, we need to ask why a society should emphasize an idealized version of social processes more than the real processes themselves. The discrepancy between the two might provide a clue to the uses which the ideology may serve.

There may be other sorts of discrepancies as well. A set of beliefs may be espoused or adhered to differently by different subgroups of the society. In the Highlands case, older men do not seem to "practice what they preach" to younger men about the dangers of association with women.

An ideology may benefit some people or groups of people in a society more than others. In the Highlands, as we have seen, older men are able to retain control over production and distribution, and over the political alignment of the local society, partially by frightening younger men away from women through the use of ideology about women.

In this case, we are speaking of the use to which a specific ideology, with a particular content, is put. But ideology per se, apart from its content, may also serve certain social functions. I have argued that ideology in the Highlands helps to constrain individuals in the absence of laws, rigidly held standards of normal and deviant behavior, or social sanctions against extreme forms of behavior. Ideology is also used in the Highlands to control women and their labor. As well, ideology is used to resolve structural stresses among men, and to reinforce a feeling of solidarity among them.

It can be quite useful to ask some of the same questions about ideology with reference to other societies. Whose purposes does it serve? Does it aid the interests of one subgroup of a society more than others? Does it represent accurately the reality of social and economic processes, or if not, why not? Does it help to resolve stresses in the social structure, to encourage a feeling of cohesion, to obscure an inequality of contribution to production or access to distribution?

Of course, ideology will be seen to function differently in each society, depending on other factors in the economic and social structure, and other questions may be more relevant.

But it is probably always useful to look behind the apparent meaning of an ideology.

III

In another avenue of inquiry, we have seen that the fluidity of social alignment has important ramifications throughout the social and economic structure of New Guinea Highland society. The fluctuation in group composition and personnel, in alliance, leadership, exchange, loyalty, and enmity, has an effect on nearly every aspect of Highland society. In some ways, the "fluidity" is like machine oil helping the gears of the society to mesh, yet the fluidity is so much a part of the structure that it is almost like another cog in the gears – that is, part of the structure itself as well as part of its functioning.

Throughout the argument of this book, I have traced the ramifications of fluidity through various aspects of social organization, an exercise in seeing the interdigitated forms of social, political, economic, and conceptual organization of a small-scale society as a more or less integrated system.

Some of the fundamental economic causes for the instability of alignment include the possibility for continual expansion in the past, and for redistribution of limited resources in the present, as well as the lack of storable food and the lack of capital formation, with its attendant rigidity of inheritance and protection. Unstable social alignments in turn contribute to the escalation of exchange and competition, especially for prestige, and increase the need for women's labor.

In terms of political organization, fluidity may be caused by warfare, but it also causes warfare. Fluctuating alliances and loyalties are both caused by, and facilitate, fission and fusion of groups involved in warfare. The lack of formal institutions of authority and for adjudication of disputes reinforces the necessity for charismatic leadership, and leads to increased political competition among big men, which in turn encourages factionalism.

Social organization is of course profoundly affected by being inherently unstable. Structural stresses (such as those between siblings, older and younger men, affines and agnates, outsiders and natal members of a local group) are aggravated because of fluctuating personnel and because of the latitude for fission. Yet in the face of the actual situation of fluid social alignment, there is a need for a feeling of cohesion among men of the local group, in order to facilitate ceremonial exchange, and because they are sometimes threatened as a unit from without, by feuding enemy groups.

The tension between the fluidity of social organization and the need for cohesion is resolved in part by various forms of ideology, as we have seen.

Similarly, the absence of formal authority, and the opportunities created by shifting social alignments, in combination with other aspects of economic and socio-political organization, give rise to a range of personality characteristics, which allow individual men to maximize their advantage in such a situation.

The paucity of structural constraints on the behavior of individuals also gives rise to the need to persuade and impress others, in order to influence what they do.

In sum, we can see that the fluctuating character of social alignment affects nearly every aspect of the structure and functioning of Highland society, from the economy to the psychology of Highland people. The ramifications of fluid social structure have an interlocking set of relationships with one another, however, which make it quite difficult at times to sort out cause and effect. For example, we could say that given the socio-economic structure, a set of personality characteristics results; but on the other hand, given the personality characteristics of Highland men, more fission and fluctuation seem the inevitable result.

Problems of this sort probably typify the search for cause and effect in small social systems, though, and they should not prompt us to give up in principle, or in despair.

IV

The "war between the sexes" has interested most people at least since the time of Aristophanes, if not before. It is no wonder that the flamboyant character of the relations between men and women in the Highlands is intriguing. But do these pyrotechnics shed any light on American society? In their disquieting glow, is there anything which illuminates the problematical relationship between the sexes which we see all around us?

Strangely enough, the respect in which the societies of the New Guinea Highlands most resemble our own seems to be in the personality of adult men. Once again, Highland society seems to echo or even caricature elements of American society: the forceful, invincible, maneuvering, and self-assured personality of Highland men is an exaggerated form of a certain ideal of manly behavior in our own society.

The resemblance is strange at first consideration, because personality is more or less at the end of the intertwined causal chain I have presented of economic and societal factors. The technological infrastructure of Highland society, as well as its economic, political, and social organization, obviously differ from our own almost as much as anything could. How could the similarities of personality style be anything other than coincidental?

Yet on closer examination we can see that in some ways the Highlands and American society have quite a bit in common, not so much in the structure or infrastructure of the society, as in the way the structure meshes, or more precisely, the way in which it slips.

Both American and Highland society are characterized by a certain fluidity in the structure's functioning, and even in the structure itself. Both societies lack a rigidly fixed hierarchy of social "slots" which only some people may occupy, and both lack a relatively inflexible inherited social status, such as that more typical of European and Asian societies.

Probably because of the opportunity for achieved status, the individual man (and in our own society, the individual woman as well) in both societies is often the center of a unique network of alliances, not an interchangeable member of a collectivity. The individual has the opportunity, and even the necessity, to restructure repeatedly his alliances and economic relationships, and in fact *must* maintain a unique set of alliances, which represent the unique intersection of many different units of sentiment, production, distribution, voluntary affiliation, kin, and so forth.

Conclusion

Of course, the social structure of the United States is not in a constant state of flux - as measured for example by the occupation and income of fathers and sons. But there are many rags-to-riches exceptions, and upward mobility on a less dramatic scale is a commonplace. The idea of the self-made man, and the idea of free competition in the competitive market, form an important part of our society's folklore and mythology, and of its personality ideals.

In both Highland society and our own, individuals are often not constrained by rigidly held societal notions about what is proper and improper behavior, as they are in older, more structurally inflexible and tradition-bound societies. In both New Guinea Highland society and American society, there is frequently a conflict between what is good for an individual and what is good for the society of which he is a part.

All of these structural characteristics, most importantly the possibility for achieved status, encourage a spirit of individualism and entrepreneurship in both New Guinea Highland society and American society, and call forth a range of "suitable" personality characteristics.

Men of both societies are often rewarded economically and socially for aggressiveness, opportunism, and subtle or unsubtle self-aggrandizement. The ability to take advantage of the moment, of openings left by a shifting social and economic structure, and to present an unchallangeable *persona* while doing so, is rewarding in Highland society and in our own.

In both societies, a great interest in material possessions dominates the desires of most people, and social status is measured, in most circles, by what is owned. Obviously there are differences between the two societies. In the Highlands the standard of personal consumption is not much increased by personal wealth, whereas in the United States, increased personal consumption is one of the chief motivations for the acquisition of material wealth. But in both societies possessions are not simply themselves, but a symbol of "success."

Of course, not everyone conforms to the idealized norm of "masculine" behavior in New Guinea Highland society, nor in our own, where the norm may become passé in some circles, and may even be adopted by women in other circles (such as in business and law).

In American society, there are other factors which have contributed to the formation of the idealized norm of masculine behavior as well. Historical circumstances, such as the meeting of English, European, and other cultures, have played an important role. So have economic factors such as historical expansion along a frontier, a constantly expanding economy, and the encouragement of competition and individualism, to which we could apply the same kind of analysis as was done with the Highlands. But these arguments will have to await another context.

The relationship between men and women in our own society, and the causal factors which influence it, are undoubtedly more complex than in New Guinea Highland society, and we have seen that to unravel those strands of causation is difficult enough.

But in both cases, we cannot understand the relationship between men and women without finding out why each sex, looked at separately, has the normative personality characteristics assigned to it by society, and we may find that the methods which were used to analyze New Guinea Highland society shed some light on our own as well.

V

Finally, we have seen that there is often a great need for better understanding of the theory underlying an explanation. Using the explanation of aversion toward women in terms of population regulation as a case in point, I showed that there are numerous issues tacit in the argument which are not well articulated in themselves, and which stand in the way of a thorough-going explanation. The way in which the explanation and theory were taken apart and examined might be applied advantageously to other kinds of explanations as well.

Such notions as carrying capacity, the assessment of population pressure, the relationship between population pressure and societal phenomena, and the relationship between population pressure and individual reproduction, are in need of further clarification in order to support explanations given in terms of population regulation.

Conclusion

Other underlying issues offer interesting avenues for new research, such as the social structural aspect of the relationship between the sexes and its influence on reproductive patterns, and the relationship between ideology about the sexes and population regulation. Perhaps the most difficult issue is the question of how to frame, descriptively and analytically, the relationship of the ideational to biological adaptation, including the regulation of population size.

One crucial notion was the subject of particular scrutiny, partly to serve as an example of the length to which an analysis of the underlying theory must sometimes be taken. I gave the notion of cultural adaptation the third degree, so to speak, because it is used to underpin many current arguments, without being very well articulated on its own. Problems in the theory of societal adaptation such as the mechanism of selection, the meaning of adaptive "success," the conflict between the "adaptations" of different overlapping units in society, and the flawed analogy with the Darwinian notion of adaptation, are especially puzzling.

Problems such as these highlight the necessity in anthropology for various types of explanation to be made more explicit, and for more discussion of the theories on which different types of explanations - economic, political, social structural, psychological, and ideational, as well as ecological - are based.

If the underlying theory remains tacit, it is possible that each new argument might have an ad hoc explanation (and even an ad hoc implicit theory). We need more discussion of the terms themselves in which our explanations are offered, to fortify both the explanation and its supporting theory. We need more agreement - or at least discussion - about the order of causation implied in various theories. Theories which explicitly spell out a hierarchy of causation, a clear definition of terms, and set of relations among elements within the theory, are taken for granted in the physical sciences. There is no reason in principle that such specificity is beyond the scope of the social sciences. But we cannot even begin to reach an agreement if we take for granted the implications of the terms we are using.

In a nineteenth century joke, a recruit complains that he does not like war. The captain answers: "Why don't you get a cannon, and go into business for yourself?" Despite the relentless spirit of entrepreneurial individualism which pervades both New Guinea Highland society and our own, we ought not, as scientists presumably looking for a common truth, each get our own theory and go into business for ourselves.

Bibliography

Alland, Alexander. 1975. "Adaptation." *Annual Review of Anthropology* 4:59-73.

Alland, Alexander and Bonnie McCay. 1973. "The Concept of Adaptation in Biological and Cultural Evolution." In *Handbook of Social and Cultural Anthropology*. John J. Honigmann, ed. Chicago: Rand McNally and Co. pp. 143-178.

Allen, M.R. 1967. *Male Cults and Secret Initiations in Melanesia*. Melbourne: Melbourne University Press.

Asad, Talal. 1979. "Anthropology and the Analysis of Ideology." *Man* n.s. 14:607-627.

Back, Kurt W. and Paula Hass. 1973. "Family Structure and Fertility Control." In *Psychological Perspectives on Population*. James T. Fawcett, et al., eds. New York: Basic Books. pp. 77-105.

Barnes, J.A. 1962. "African Models in the New Guinea Highlands." *Man* 62:5-9.

Barth, Frederik. 1975. *Ritual and Knowledge Among the Baktaman of New Guinea*. New Haven: Yale University Press.

Bateson, Gregory. 1958, originally 1936. *Naven*, second edition. Stanford: Stanford University Press.

Bayliss-Smith, Tim. 1974. "Constraints on Population Growth: The Case of the Polynesian Outlier Atolls in the Precontact Period." *Human Ecology* 2:259-295.

Berndt, Catherine H. 1966. "The Ghost Husband: Society and the Individual in New Guinea Myth." *Journal of American Folklore* 79:244-277.

Berndt, Ronald M. 1962. *Excess and Restraint: Social Control Among a New Guinea Mountain People*. Chicago: University of Chicago Press.

_____. 1965. "The Kamano, Jate, Usurufa, and Fore of the Eastern Highlands." In *Gods, Ghosts, and Men in Melanesia: Some Religions of Australian New Guinea and the New Hebrides*. P. Lawrence and M.J. Meggitt, eds. Melbourne: Oxford University Press. pp. 78-104.

_____. 1969. "Political Structure in the Eastern Central Highlands of New Guinea." *Anthropological Forum* 2:327-369.

Berryman, Alan A. 1981. *Population Systems: A General Introduction*. New York: Plenum Press.

Berthoud, Gérald. 1974. "La Signification Sociale des 'Biens de Prestige' dans les Formations Lignagères Africaines." *Canadian Journal of African Studies* 8:307-324.

Biersack, Aletta. 1984. "Paiela 'women-men': the reflexive foundations of gender ideology." *American Ethnologist* 11:118-139.

Bohannan, Paul and Laura Bohannan. 1968. *Tiv Economy.* Evanston, Illinois: Northwestern University Press.

Bowers, Nancy. 1965. "Permanent Bachelorhood in the Upper Kaugel Valley of Highland New Guinea." *Oceania* 36:27-37.

_____. 1971. "Demographic Problems in Montane New Guinea." In *Culture and Population: A Collection of Current Studies.* Steven Polgar, ed. Cambridge, Mass.: Carolina Population Center, distributed by Shenkman Publishing Co., Inc. pp. 11-31.

Brandewie, Ernst. 1971. "The Place of the Big Man in Traditional Hagen Society in the Central Highlands of New Guinea." *Ethnology* 10:194-210.

Brandon, Robert N. 1984a. "Adaptation and Evolutionary Theory." In *Conceptual Issues in Evolutionary Biology: An Anthology.* Elliot Sober, ed. Cambridge: MIT Press. pp. 58-82.

_____. 1984b. "The Levels of Selection." In *Genes, Organisms, Populations: Controversies over the Units of Selection.* Robert N. Brandon and Richard M. Burian, eds. Cambridge: MIT Press. pp. 133-141.

_____. 1985. "Adaptation Explanations: Are Adaptations for the Good of Replicators or Interactors?" In *Evolution at a Crossroads: The New Biology and the New Philosophy of Science.* David J. Depew and Bruce H. Weber, eds. Cambridge: MIT Press. pp. 81-96.

Brandon, Robert N. and Richard M. Burian, eds. 1984. *Genes, Organisms, Populations: Controversies over the Units of Selection.* Cambridge: MIT Press.

Brookfield, H.C. 1959. "Two Population Problem Areas of Papua New Guinea." *South Pacific* 10:133-137.

_____. 1961. "The Highland Peoples of New Guinea: A Study of Distribution and Localization." *Geographical Journal* 127:434-448.

_____. 1962. "Local Study and Comparative Method: An Example from Central New Guinea." *Annals of the Association of American Geographers* 52:242-254.

_____. 1964. "The Ecology of Highland Settlement: Some Suggestions." *American Anthropologist* 66:20-38.

Brookfield, H.C. and Paula Brown. 1963. *Struggle for Land: Agriculture and Group Territories among the Chimbu of the New Guinea Highlands.* Melbourne: Oxford University Press.

Bibliography

Brookfield, H.C. and J. Peter White. 1968. "Revolution or Evolution in the Prehistory of the New Guinea Highlands: A Seminar Report." *Ethnology* 7:43-52.

Brown, Paula. 1962. "Non-Agnates among the Patrilineal Chimbu." *The Journal of the Polynesian Society* 71:57-69.

_____. 1964. "Enemies and Affines." *Ethnology* 3:335-356.

_____. 1967. "The Chimbu Political System." *Anthropological Forum* 2:36-52.

_____. 1969. "Marriage in Chimbu." In *Pigs, Pearlshells, and Women: Marriage in the New Guinea Highlands*. R.M. Glasse and M.J. Meggitt, eds. Englewood Cliffs, New Jersey: Prentice-Hall, Inc. pp. 77-95.

_____. 1970. "Chimbu Transactions." *Man* n.s. 5:99-117.

_____. 1972. *The Chimbu: A Study of Change in the New Guinea Highlands*. Cambridge, Mass.: Shenkman Publishing Co., Inc.

_____. 1978. "New Guinea: Ecology, Society, and Culture." *Annual Review of Anthropology* 7:263-291.

Brown, Paula and Georgeda Buchbinder. 1976. "Introduction." In *Man and Woman in the New Guinea Highlands*. Paula Brown and Georgeda Buchbinder, eds. Washington, D.C.: American Anthropological Association. pp. 1-12.

Brown, Paula and Aaron Podolefsky. 1976. "Population Density, Agricultural Intensity, and Group Size in the New Guinea Highlands." *Ethnology* 15:211-238.

Brush, Stephen B. 1975. "The Concept of Carrying Capacity for Systems of Shifting Cultivation." *American Anthropologist* 77:799-811.

Buchbinder, Georgeda and Roy Rappaport. 1976. "Fertility and Death among the Maring." In *Man and Woman in the NGH*. Brown and Buchbinder, eds., op. cit. pp. 13-35.

Bulmer, Ralph. 1960. "Political Aspects of the Moka Ceremonial Exchange System among the Kyaka People of the Western Highlands of New Guinea." *Oceania* 31:1-13.

_____. 1965. "The Kyaka of the Western Highlands." In *Gods, Ghosts, and Men*. Lawrence and Meggitt, eds., op. cit. pp. 132-161.

_____. 1968. "The Strategies of Hunting in New Guinea." *Oceania* 38:302-318.

_____. 1971. "Traditional Forms of Family Limitation in New Guinea." *New Guinea Research Bulletin* 42:137-162.

Bulmer, Ralph and Susan Bulmer. 1964. "The Prehistory of the Australian New Guinea Highlands." *American Anthropologist* 66:39-76.

Burton, Roger V. and John W.M. Whiting. 1961. "The Absent Father and Cross-Sex Identity." *Merrill-Palmer Quarterly of Behavior and Development* 7:85-95.

Chowning, Ann. 1969. "The Fertility of Melanesian Girls, Laboratory Mice, and Prostitutes: A Comment on the Bruce Effect." *American Anthropologist* 71:1122-1123.

Clarke, William. 1971. *Place and People: An Ecology of a New Guinean Community.* Berkeley: University of California Press.

Cohen, Mark N. 1980. "Speculations on the Evolution of Density Measurement and Population Regulation in *Homo Sapiens.*" In *Biosocial Mechanisms of Population Regulation.* Mark Nathan Cohen, Roy S. Malpass, and Harold G. Klein, eds. New Haven: Yale University Press. pp. 275-303.

Collier, Jane Fishburne. 1974. "Women in Politics." In *Woman, Culture and Society.* Michelle Z. Rosaldo and Louise Lamphere, eds. Stanford: Stanford University Press. pp. 89-96.

Collier, Jane F. and Michelle Z. Rosaldo. 1981. "Politics and gender in simple societies." In *Sexual Meanings: The Cultural Construction of Gender and Sexuality.* Sherry B. Ortner and Harriet Whitehead, eds. Cambridge: Cambridge University Press. pp. 275-329.

Cook, E.A. 1969. "Marriage among the Manga." In *Pigs, Pearlshells, and Women.* Glasse and Meggitt, eds., op. cit. pp. 96-116.

Dalton, George. 1967. "Primitive Money." In *Tribal and Peasant Economies: Readings in Economic Anthropology.* George Dalton, ed. Garden City, New York: The Natural History Press. pp. 254-281.

Denitch, Bette S. 1974. "Sex and Power in the Balkans." In *Woman, Culture, and Society.* Rosaldo and Lamphere, eds., op. cit. pp. 243-262.

Dewar, Robert E. 1984. "Environmental Productivity, Population Regulation, and Carrying Capacity." *American Anthropologist* 86:601-614.

Divale, William T. 1970. "An Explanation for Primitive Warfare: Population Controls and the Significance of Primitive Sex Ratios." *The New Scholar* 2:173-192.

_____. 1972. "Systemic Population Control in the Middle and Upper Paleolithic: Inferences Based on Contemporary Hunter-Gatherers." *World Archaeology* 4:222-243.

Divale, William T. and Marvin Harris. 1976. "Population, Warfare, and the Male Supremacist Complex." *American Anthropologist* 78:521-538.

Dornstreich, Mark D. and George E.B. Morren, Jr. 1974. "Does New Guinea Cannibalism Have a Nutritional Value?" *Human Ecology* 2:1-12.

Douglas, Mary. 1966a. "Population Control in Primitive Societies." *British Journal of Sociology* 17:263-273.

Bibliography

_____. 1966b. *Purity and Danger*. Middlesex, England: Penguin Books, Ltd.

_____. 1967a. "Primitive Rationing: A Study in Controlled Exchange." In *Themes in Economic Anthropology*. Raymond Firth, ed. London: Tavistock Publications. pp. 119-107.

_____. 1967b. "Raffia Cloth Distribution in the Lele Economy." In *Tribal and Peasant Economies*. Dalton, ed., op. cit. pp. 103-122.

DuBois, Cora. 1936. "The Wealth Concept as an Integrating Factor in Tolowa-Tutuni Culture." In *Essays in Anthropology Presented to A.L. Kroeber in Celebration of his Sixtieth Birthday*. Robert H. Lowie, ed. Freeport, New York: Books for Libraries Press, Inc. pp. 49-65.

Elkin, A.P. 1953. "Delayed Exchange in Wabag Sub-District, Central Highlands of New Guinea." *Oceania* 23:161-201.

Faithorn, Elizabeth. 1975. "The Concept of Pollution among the Kafe of the Papua New Guinea Highlands." In *Toward an Anthropology of Women*. Rayna Reiter, ed. New York: Monthly Review Press. pp. 127-140.

_____. 1976. "Women as Persons: Aspects of Female Life and Male-Female Relations among the Kafe." In *Man and Woman in the NGH*. Brown and Buchbinder, eds., op. cit. pp. 86-95.

Feil, D.K. 1978a. "'Straightening the way': an Enga kinship conundrum." *Man* n.s. 13:380-401.

_____. 1978b. "Women and Men in the Enga Tee." *American Ethnologist* 5:263-279.

_____. 1980. "Symmetry and Complementarity: Patterns of Competition and Exchange in the Enga Tee." *Oceania* 51:20-39.

_____. 1986. "A Social Anthropologist's View of Papua New Guinea Highlands Prehistory." *American Anthropologist* 88:623-636.

Firth, Raymond. 1967. "Themes in Economic Anthropology." In *Themes in Economic Anthropology*. Firth, ed., op. cit. pp. 1-28.

Frankenburg, Ronald. 1967. "Economic Anthropology: One Anthropologist's View." In *Themes in Economic Anthropology*. Firth, ed., op. cit. pp. 47-90.

Gelber, Marilyn G. n.d. "The Concept of Prestige and its Operation in the New Guinea Highlands." ms.

_____. n.d. "The Social Structure of the Relationship between Men and Women in Jamaica and its Effect on Reproduction." ms.

Gell, A.F. 1971. "Penis Sheathing and Ritual Status in a West Sepik Village." *Man* n.s. 6:165-181.

George, Peter. 1963. *Dr. Strangelove or: How I Learned to Stop Worrying and Love the Bomb*, a novel based on the screenplay by Stanley Kubrick, Peter George, and Terry Southern. New York: Bantam Books, Inc.

Gillison, Gillian. 1980. "Images of Nature in Gimi Thought." In *Nature, Culture, and Gender.* Carol MacCormack and Marilyn Strathern, eds. Cambridge: Cambridge University Press. pp. 143-173.

Gitlow, Abraham. 1947. *Economics of the Mt. Hagen Tribes, New Guinea.* Monographs of the American Ethnological Society.

Glasse, Robert M. 1965. "The Huli of the Southern Highlands." In *Gods, Ghosts, and Men.* Lawrence and Meggitt, eds., op. cit. pp. 27-49.

────────. 1968. *Huli of Papua: A Cognatic Descent System.* Paris: Mouton and Co.

────────. 1969. "Marriage in South Fore." In *Pigs, Pearlshells, and Women.* Glasse and Meggitt, eds., op. cit. pp. 16-37.

────────. 1974. "Le Masque de la Volupté: Symbolisme et Antagonisme sur les Hauts Plateaus de Nouvelle Guinée." *L'Homme* 14:79-86.

────────. n.d. "Volcanoes and Virtue: An Analysis of Sexual Symbols and Population Controls." ms.

Glasse, Robert M. and Mervyn J. Meggitt, eds. 1969. *Pigs, Pearlshells, and Women: Marriage in the New Guinea Highlands.* New Jersey: Prentice-Hall, Inc.

Godelier, Maurice. 1971. "'Salt Currency' and the Circulation of Commodities among the Baruya of New Guinea." In *Studies in Economic Anthropology.* George Dalton, ed. Washington, D.C.: American Anthropological Association. pp. 52-73.

────────. 1982. "Social Hierarchies among the Baruya of New Guinea." In *Inequality in New Guinea Highland Societies.* Andrew Strathern, ed. Cambridge: Cambridge University Press. pp. 3-34.

Godelier, Maurice and José Garanger. 1973. "Outils de Pierre, Outils d'Acier chez les Baruya de Nouvelle Guinée." *L'Homme* 13:187-220.

Gould, Stephen J. and Richard C. Lewontin. 1984. "The Spandrels of San Marco and the Panglossian Paradigm: A Critique of the Adaptationist Programme." In *Conceptual Issues.* Elliot Sober, ed., op. cit. pp. 252-270.

Hallpike, C.R. 1977. *Bloodshed and Vengeance in the Papuan Mountains: The Generation of Conflict in Tauade Society.* Oxford: Oxford University Press.

Harris, G.T. 1978. "Responses to Population Pressure in the Papua New Guinea Highlands, 1957-1974." *Oceania* 48:284-298.

Hassan, Fekri A. 1973. "On Mechanisms of Population Growth During the Neolithic." *Current Anthropology* 14:535-542.

_____. 1980. "The Growth and Regulation of Human Population in Prehistoric Times." In *Biosocial Mechanisms*. M.N. Cohen et al, eds., op. cit. pp. 305-319.

_____. 1981. *Demographic Archaeology*. New York: Academic Press.

Hayano, David M. 1974. "Marriage, Alliance, and Warfare: A View from the New Guinea Highlands." *American Ethnologist* 1:281-293.

Hays, Terence E. and Patricia H. Hays. 1982. "Opposition and Complementarity of the Sexes in Ndumba Initiation." In *Rituals of Manhood: Male Initiation in Papua New Guinea*. Gilbert Herdt, ed. Berkeley: University of California Press. pp. 201-238.

Hayden, Brian. 1972. "Population Control among Hunter Gatherers." *World Archaeology* 4:205-222.

Healey, Christopher H. 1978. "The Adaptive Significance of Systems of Ceremonial Exchange and Trade in the New Guinea Highlands." *Mankind* 11:198-207.

Heider, Karl. 1970. *The Dugum Dani: A Papuan Culture in the Highlands of West New Guinea*. Chicago: Aldine Publishing Company.

Hempel, Carl G. 1965. "The Logic of Functional Analysis." In *Aspects of Scientific Explanation and Other Essays in the Philosophy of Science*. Carl G. Hempel. New York: The Free Press. pp. 297-330.

Herdt, Gilbert H. 1981. *Guardians of the Flutes: Idioms of Masculinity*. New York: McGraw-Hill.

_____. 1982. "Fetish and Fantasy in Sambia Initiation." In *Rituals of Manhood*. Herdt, ed., op. cit. pp. 44-98.

_____. 1984. "Ritualized Homosexual Behavior in the Male Cults of Melanesia, 1862-1983: An Introduction." In *Ritualized Homosexuality in Melanesia*. Gilbert Herdt, ed. Berkeley: University of California Press. pp. 1-81.

Herdt, Gilbert H. and Fitz John P. Poole. 1982. "Sexual Antagonism: The Intellectual History of a Concept in New Guinea Anthropology." *Social Analysis* 12:3-28.

Hipsley, Eben E. and Nancy E. Kirk. 1965. *Studies of Dietary Intake and the Expenditure of Energy by New Guineans*. South Pacific Commission Technical Paper #147. Sydney, Australia: G.P.O.

Hull, David. 1984. "Units of Evolution: A Metaphysical Essay." In *Genes, Organisms, Populations*. Brandon and Burian, eds., op. cit. pp. 142-160.

Johnson, Patricia Lyons. 1981. "When Dying is Better than Living: Female Suicide among the Gainj of Papua New Guinea." *Ethnology* 20:325-334.

Josephides, Lisette. 1983. "Equal but Different? The Ontology of Gender among Kewa." *Oceania* 53:291-307.

---. 1985. *The Production of Inequality: Gender and Exchange among the Kewa*. London: Tavistock.
Kaberry, Phyllis M. 1967. "The Plasticity of New Guinea Kinship." In *Social Organization: Essays Presented to Raymond Firth*. Maurice Freedman, ed. London: Frank Cass and Co., Ltd. pp. 105-123.
Kaplan, David and Robert A. Manners. 1972. *Culture Theory*. Englewood Cliffs, New Jersey: Prentice-Hall.
Keesing, Roger M. 1982. "Introduction." In *Rituals of Manhood*. Herdt, ed., op. cit. pp. 2-43.
Kelly, Raymond C. 1968. "Demographic Pressure and Descent Group Structure in the New Guinea Highlands." *Oceania* 39:36-63.
---. 1974. *Etoro Social Structure: A Study in Structural Contradiction*. Ann Arbor: The University of Michigan Press.
---. 1976. "Witchcraft and Sexual Relations: An Exploration in the Social and Semantic Implications of the Structure of Belief." In *Man and Woman in the NGH*. Brown and Buchbinder, eds., op. cit. pp. 36-53.
King, James C. 1980. "The Genetics of Sociobiology." In *Sociobiology Examined*. Ashley Montagu, ed. Oxford: Oxford University Press. pp. 82-107.
Koch, Klaus-Friedrich. 1968a. "Marriage in Jalemo." *Oceania* 39:85-109.
---. 1968b. "On 'Possession' Behavior in New Guinea." *Journal of the Polynesian Society* 77:135-146.
---. 1974. "Sociogenic and Psychogenic Models in Anthropology: The Functions of Jale Initiation." *Man* n.s. 9:397-422.
Kracke, Waud H. 1980. "The Complementarity of Social and Psychological Regularities: Leadership as a Mediating Phenomenon." *Ethos* 8:273-285.
Lamphere, Louise. 1974. "Strategies, Cooperation, and Conflict among Women in Domestic Groups." In *Woman, Culture, and Society*. Rosaldo and Lamphere, eds., op. cit. pp. 97-112.
Langness, L. 1964. "Some Problems in the Conceptualization of Highlands Social Structures." *American Anthropologist* 66:162-182.
---. 1965. "Hysterical Psychosis in the New Guinea Highlands: A Bena Bena Example." *Psychiatry* 28:258-277.
---. 1967a. "Hysterical Psychosis: The Cross Cultural Evidence." *American Journal of Psychiatry* 124:143-152.
---. 1967b. "Sexual Antagonism in the New Guinea Highlands: A Bena Bena Example." *Oceania* 37:161-177.
---. 1969. "Marriage in Bena Bena." In *Pigs, Pearlshells, and Women*. Glasse and Meggitt eds., op. cit. pp. 38-55.

_____. 1974. "Ritual, Power, and Male Dominance." *Ethos* 2:189-212.

_____. 1976. "Discussion." In *Man and Woman in the NGH*. Brown and Buchbinder, eds., op. cit. pp. 96-106.

Lawrence, P. and M.J. Meggitt. 1965. "Introduction." In *Gods, Ghosts, and Men*. Lawrence and Meggitt, eds., op. cit. pp. 1-25.

Lee, Richard B. 1980. "Lactation, Ovulation, Infanticide, and Women's Work: A Study of Hunter-Gatherer Population Regulation." In *Biosocial Mechanisms*. M.N. Cohen, et al, eds., op. cit. pp. 321-348.

de Lepervanche, Marie. 1967. "Descent, Residence, and Leadership in the New Guinea Highlands." *Oceania* 38:134-158.

_____. 1968. "Descent, Residence, and Leadership in the New Guinea Highlands" (continued). *Oceania* 38:163-189.

LeVine, Robert A. 1973. *Culture, Behavior, and Personality*. Chicago: Aldine.

Lewontin, Richard C. 1978. "Adaptation." *Scientific American* 239:212-230.

_____. 1984. "Adaptation." In *Conceptual Issues*. Elliot Sober, ed., op. cit. pp. 210-231.

Lindenbaum, Shirley. 1972. "Sorcerers, Ghosts, and Polluting Women: An Analysis of Religious Belief and Population Control." *Ethnology* 2:241-253.

_____. 1976. "A Wife is the Hand of Man." In *Man and Woman in the NGH*. Brown and Buchbinder, eds., op. cit. pp. 54-62.

_____. 1979. *Kuru Sorcery: Disease and Danger in the New Guinea Highlands*. Palo Alto: Mayfield Publishing Company.

LiPuma, Edward. 1978. "Sexual Asymmetry and Social Reproduction among the Maring of Papua New Guinea." *Ethnos* 43:34-57.

Lowman-Vayda, Cherry. 1968. "Maring Big Men." *Anthropological Forum* 2:199-243.

Malinowski, Bronislaw. 1967, originally 1920. "Kula: The Circulating Exchange of Valuables in the Archipelagoes of Eastern New Guinea." In *Tribal and Peasant Economies*. Dalton, ed., op. cit. pp. 171-184. (originally published in *Man* 1920).

Mandeville, Elizabeth. 1979. "Agnation, Affinity, and Migration among the Kamano of the New Guinea Highlands." *Man* n.s. 14:105-123.

Martin, Paul S. 1973. "The Discovery of America." *Science* 179:969-974.

Maybury-Lewis, David H.P. 1967. *Akwĕ-Shavante Society*. Oxford: Clarendon Press.

Medawar, P.B. 1981. "Stretch Genes." (A Review of Genes, Mind, and Culture: The Co-Evolutionary Process, by Charles J. Lumsden and Edward O. Wilson). *The New York Review of Books*, July 16, 1981. pp. 45-58.

Meggitt, Mervyn J. 1964. "Male-Female Relationships in the Highlands of Australian New Guinea." *American Anthropologist* 66:204-224.

_____. 1965a. *The Lineage System of the Mae Enga of New Guinea*. Edinburgh: Oliver and Boyd.

_____. 1965b. "The Mae Enga of the Western Highlands." In *Gods, Ghosts, and Men*. Lawrence and Meggitt, eds., op. cit. pp. 105-131.

_____. 1967. "The Pattern of Leadership among the Mae Enga of New Guinea." *Anthropological Forum* 2:20-35.

_____. 1969. "Introduction." In *Pigs, Pearlshells, and Women*. Glasse and Meggitt, eds., op. cit. pp. 1-15.

_____. 1974. "Pigs are our Hearts! The Te Exchange Cycle among the Mae Enga of New Guinea." *Oceania* 44:165-203.

_____. 1976. "A Duplicity of Demons: Sexual and Familial Roles Expressed in Western Enga Stories." In *Man and Woman in the NGH*. Brown and Buchbinder, eds., op. cit. pp. 63-85.

_____. 1977. *Blood is Their Argument: Warfare among the Mae Enga Tribesmen of the New Guinea Highlands*. Palo Alto: Mayfield Publishing Company.

Meigs, Anna S. 1978. "A Papuan Perspective on Pollution." *Man* n.s. 13:304-318.

_____. 1984. *Food, Sex, and Pollution: A New Guinea Religion*. New Brunswick, New Jersey: Rutgers University Press.

Modjeska, Nicholas. 1982a. "Comment." (response to article by J. Peoples). *Current Anthropology* 23:302-303.

_____. 1982b. "Production and inequality: perspectives from Central New Guinea." In *Inequality in NGH Societies*. A. Strathern, ed., op. cit. pp. 50-108.

Montagu, Ashley. 1980. *Sociobiology Examined*. Oxford: Oxford University Press.

Murphy, Robert F. 1959. "Social Structure and Sex Antagonism." *Southwestern Journal of Anthropology* 15:89-98.

Murray, Bertram G., Jr. 1979. *Population Dynamics: Alternative Models*. New York: Academic Press.

Nagel, Ernest. 1961. *The Structure of Science: Problems in the Logic of Scientific Explanation*. New York: Harcourt, Brace, and World.

Newman, Philip L. 1964a. "Religious Belief and Ritual in a New Guinea Society." *American Anthropologist* 66:257-272.

_____. 1964b. "'Wild Man' Behavior in a New Guinea Highlands Community." *American Anthropologist* 66:1-19.

Bibliography

_____. 1965. *Knowing the Gururumba.* New York: Holt, Rinehart, and Winston.

Newman, Philip L. and David J. Boyd. 1982. "The Making of Men: Ritual and Meaning in Awa Male Initiation." In *Rituals of Manhood.* Gilbert Herdt, ed., op. cit. pp. 239-285.

Nishiyama, Ichizo. 1963. "The Origin of the Sweet Potato Plant." In *Plants and the Migration of Pacific Peoples.* Jacques Barrau, ed. Honolulu: Bishop Museum Press. pp. 119-128.

O'Brien, Denise. 1984. "'Women Never Hunt': The Portrayal of Women in Melanesian Society." In *Rethinking Women's Roles: Perspectives from the Pacific.* Denise O'Brien and Sharon W. Tiffany, eds. Berkeley: University of California Press. pp. 53-70.

Olson, Mancur. 1965. *The Logic of Collective Action.* Cambridge: Harvard University Press.

Oosterwal, G. 1959. "The Position of the Bachelor in the Upper Tor Territory." *American Anthropologist* 61:828-838.

Orlove, Benjamin S. 1980. "Ecological Anthropology." *Annual Review of Anthropology* 9:235-273.

Peoples, James G. 1982. "Individual or Group Advantage? A Reinterpretation of the Maring Ritual Cycle." *Current Anthropology* 23:291-300.

Polanyi, Karl. 1968. "The Economy as Instituted Process." In *Economic Anthropology: Readings in Theory and Analysis.* Edward W. LeClair and Harold K. Schneider, eds. New York: Holt, Rinehart, and Winston. pp. 122-143.

Poole, Fitz John Porter. 1982. "The Ritual Forging of Identity: Aspects of Person and Self in Bimin-Kuskusmin Male Initiation." In *Rituals of Manhood.* Herdt, ed., op. cit. pp. 99-154.

Pospisil, Leopold. 1963a. *Kapauku Papuan Economy.* New Haven: Yale University Publications in Anthropology #67.

_____. 1963b. *The Kapauku Papuans of West New Guinea.* New York: Holt, Rinehart, and Winston.

Powell, Dorian, L. Hewitt, and P. Woo Ming. 1978. "Contraceptive Use in Jamaica: the Social, Economic, and Cultural Context." University of the West Indies Institute of Social and Economic Research: Working Paper #19.

Rappaport, Roy A. 1968. *Pigs for the Ancestors: Ritual in the Ecology of a New Guinea People.* New Haven: Yale University Press.

_____. 1969. "Marriage among the Maring." In *Pigs, Pearlshells, and Women.* Glasse and Meggitt, eds., op. cit. pp. 117-137.

_____. 1978a. "Maladaptation in Social Systems." In *The Evolution of Social Systems.* J. Friedman and M.J. Rowlands, eds. Pittsburgh: The University of Pittsburgh Press. pp. 49-71.

_____. 1978b. "Normative Models of Adaptive Processes: A Response to Anne Whyte." In *Evolution of Social Systems.* Friedman and Rowlands, eds., op. cit. pp. 79-87.

_____. 1979. "Adaptive Structure and Its Disorders." In *Ecology, Meaning, and Religion.* Roy Rappaport. Richmond, California: North Atlantic Books. pp. 145-172.

_____. 1982. "Comment." (response to article by J. Peoples). *Current Anthropology* 23:303-305.

_____. 1984. "Epilogue, 1984." In *Pigs for the Ancestors: Ritual in the Ecology of a New Guinea People,* a new, enlarged edition. New Haven: Yale University Press. pp. 299-444.

Read, Kenneth E. 1952. "Nama Cult of the Central Highlands, New Guinea." *Oceania* 23:1-25.

_____. 1954a. "Cultures of the Central Highlands, New Guinea." *Southwestern Journal of Anthropology* 10:1-43.

_____. 1954b. "Marriage among the Gahuku-Gama of the Eastern Central Highlands, New Guinea." *South Pacific* 7:864-871.

_____. 1959. "Leadership and Consensus in a New Guinea Society." *American Anthropologist* 61:425-436.

_____. 1965. *The High Valley.* New York: Charles Scribners Sons.

_____. 1982. "Male-Female Relationships among the Gahuku-Gama: 1950 and 1981." *Social Analysis* 12:66-78.

Reay, Marie. 1959a. *The Kuma: Freedom and Conformity in the New Guinea Highlands.* London: Cambridge University Press.

_____. 1959b. "Two Kinds of Ritual Conflict". *Oceania* 29:290-296.

_____. 1960. "Mushroom Madness in the New Guinea Highlands." *Oceania* 31:137-139.

_____. 1967. "Structural Co-Variants of Land Shortage Among Patrilineal Peoples." *Anthropological Forum* 2:4-19.

Riesman, Paul. n.d. "On the Irrelevance of Child Rearing Practices for the Formation of Personality: An Analysis of Childhood, Personality, and Values in two African Communities." ms.

Robbins, R.G. 1963. "Correlations of Plant Patterns and Population Migration into the Australian New Guinea Highlands." In *Plants and Migration.* Barrau, ed., op. cit. pp. 45-59.

Rodrique, Roger B. 1963. "A Report on a Widespread Psychological Disorder Called Lulu among the Huli Linguistic Group in Papua." *Oceania* 33:273-279.

Rosman, Abraham and Paula G. Rubel. 1971. *Feasting with Mine Enemy: Rank and Exchange among Northwest Coast Societies.* New York: Columbia University Press.

Ross, John Alan. 1965. "The Puberty Ceremony of the Chimbu Girl in the Eastern Highlands of New Guinea." *Anthropos* 60:423-432.

Rubel, Paula G. and Abraham Rosman. 1978. *Your Own Pigs You May Not Eat: A Comparative Study of New Guinea Societies.* Chicago: University of Chicago Press.

Ryan, D'Arcy. 1969. "Marriage in Mendi." In *Pigs, Pearlshells, and Women.* Glasse and Meggitt, eds., op. cit. pp. 159-175.

Sahlins, Marshall D. 1968. "Poor Man, Rich Man, Big Man, Chief: Political Types in Melanesia and Polynesia." In *Peoples and Cultures of the Pacific.* Andrew P. Vayda, ed. New York: The Natural History Press. pp. 157-176.

_____. 1972. "On the Sociology of Primitive Exchange." In *Stone Age Economics.* M. Sahlins. Chicago: Aldine-Atherton, Inc. pp. 185-275.

Salisbury, Richard F. 1960. "Ceremonial Economics and Political Equilibrium." *International Congress of Anthropological and Ethnological Sciences, 6th.* Paris II:255-259.

_____. 1962. *From Stone to Steel: Economic Consequences of a Technological Change in New Guinea.* Victoria: Melbourne University Press.

_____. 1965. "The Siane of the Eastern Highlands." In *Gods, Ghosts, and Men.* Lawrence and Meggitt, eds., op. cit. pp. 50-77.

_____. 1966. "Possession in the New Guinea Highlands: Review of the Literature." *Transcultural Psychiatric Research* 3:103-108.

Sanday, Peggy R. 1981. *Female Power and Male Dominance: On the Origins of Sexual Inequality.* Cambridge: Cambridge University Press.

Schieffelin, Edward L. 1976. *The Sorrow of the Lonely and the Burning of the Dancers.* New York: St. Martin's Press.

Schwartz, Theodore. 1973. "Cult and Context: The Paranoid Ethos in Melanesia." *Ethos* 1:153-174.

Schweder, Richard A. 1979. "Rethinking Culture and Personality Theory Part I: A Critical Examination of Two Classical Postulates." *Ethos* 7:255-278.

Sexton, Lorraine Dusak. 1984. "Pigs, Pearlshells, and 'Women's Work': Collective Response to Change in Highland Papua New Guinea." In *Rethinking Women's Roles.* O'Brien and Tiffany, eds., op cit. pp. 120-152.

Shedlin, Michele Goldzieher and Paula E. Hollerbach. 1981. "Modern and Traditional Fertility Regulation in a Mexican Community: The Process of Decision Making." *Studies in Family Planning* 12:278-296.

Sillitoe, Paul. 1977. "Land Shortage and War in New Guinea." *Ethnology* 16:71-81.

---------. 1979. *Give and Take: Exchange in Wola Society.* New York: St. Martin's Press.
Sinnett, P.F. and H.M. Whyte. 1973. "Epidemiological Studies in a Highland Population of New Guinea: Environment, Culture, and Health Status." *Human Ecology* 1:245-277.
Siskind, Janet. 1973. "Tropical Forest Hunters and the Economy of Sex." In *Peoples and Cultures of Native South America.* Daniel Gross, ed. Garden City, New York: Doubleday, The Natural History Press. pp. 226-240.
Sober, Elliot. 1984a. "Holism, Individualism, and the Units of Selection." In *Conceptual Issues.* Elliot Sober, ed., op. cit. pp. 184-209.
---------. 1984b. *The Nature of Selection: Evolutionary Theory in Philosophical Focus.* Cambridge: MIT Press.
Sober, Elliot, ed. 1984. *Conceptual Issues in Evolutionary Biology: An Anthology.* Section III, "The Units of Selection." Cambridge: MIT Press. pp. 117-231.
Sober, Elliot, and Richard C. Lewontin. 1984. "Artifact, Cause, and Genic Selection." In *Genes, Organisms, Populations.* Brandon and Burian, eds., op. cit. pp. 109-132.
Sorenson, E. Richard. 1972. "Socio-Ecological Change among the Fore of New Guinea." *Current Anthropology* 13:349-385.
---------. 1976. *The Edge of the Forest: Land, Childhood, and Change in a New Guinea Protoagricultural Society.* Washington, D.C.: Smithsonian Institution Press.
Sorenson, E. Richard and Peter E. Kenmore. 1974. "Proto-Agricultural Movement in the Eastern Highlands of New Guinea." *Current Anthropology* 15:67-73.
Spiro, Melford E. 1961. "Social Systems, Personality, and Functional Analysis." In *Studying Personality Cross-Culturally.* Bert Kaplan, ed. Evanston, Illinois: Row, Peterson, and Co. pp. 93-127.
Stott, D.H. 1969. "Cultural and Natural Checks on Population Growth." In *Environment and Cultural Behavior: Ecological Studies in Cultural Anthropology.* Andrew Vayda, ed. Garden City, New York: The Natural History Press. pp. 90-120.
Strathern, Andrew. 1966. "Despots and Directors." *Man* n.s. 1:356-367.
---------. 1969a. "Descent and Alliance in the New Guinea Highlands: Some Problems of Comparison." *Royal Anthropological Institute Proceedings for 1968.* pp. 37-52. Curl Prize Essay.
---------. 1969b. "Finance and Production: Two Strategies in New Guinea Highlands Exchange Systems." *Oceania* 40:42-67.
---------. 1970a. "The Female and Male Spirit Cults in Mt. Hagen." *Man* n.s. 5:571-585.

_____. 1970b. "Male Initiation in New Guinea Highland Societies." *Ethnology* 9:373-379.

_____. 1971a. "Cargo and Inflation in Mount Hagen." *Oceania* 40:42-67.

_____. 1971b. "Pig Complex and Cattle Complex: Some Comparisons and Counterpoints." *Mankind* 8:129-136.

_____. 1971c. *The Rope of Moka: Big Men and Ceremonial Exchange in Mt. Hagen, New Guinea.* Cambridge: Cambridge University Press.

_____. 1972. *One Father, One Blood: Descent and Group Structure among the Melpa People.* London: Tavistock Publications.

_____. 1973. "Kinship, Descent, and Locality: Some New Guinea Examples." In *The Character of Kinship.* Jack Goody, ed. Cambridge: Cambridge University Press. pp. 21-33.

_____. 1979a. "Gender, Ideology, and Money in Mt. Hagen." *Man* n.s. 14:530-548.

_____. 1979b. (translation). *Onka: A Self-Account by a New Guinea Big Man.* New York: St. Martin's Press.

_____. 1982. "Two Waves of African Models in the New Guinea Highlands." In *Inequality in NGH Societies.* A. Strathern, ed., op. cit. pp. 35-49.

Strathern, Andrew and Marilyn Strathern. 1969. "Marriage in Melpa." In *Pigs, Pearlshells, and Women.* Glasse and Meggitt, eds., op. cit. pp. 138-158.

_____. 1971. *Self-Decoration in Mt. Hagen.* Toronto: University of Toronto Press.

Strathern, Marilyn. 1972. *Women in Between: Female Roles in a Male World, Mt. Hagen, New Guinea.* London: Seminar Press.

_____. 1978. "The Achievement of Sex: Paradoxes in Hagen Gender-Thinking." In *Yearbook of Symbolic Anthropology.* Eric Schwimmer, ed. London: Hurst. pp. 171-202.

_____. 1980. "No nature, no culture: the Hagen case." In *Nature, Culture, and Gender.* MacCormack and M. Strathern, eds., op. cit. pp. 174-222.

_____. 1981. "Self-interest and the social good: some implications of Hagen gender imagery." In *Sexual Meanings.* Ortner and Whitehead, eds., op. cit. pp. 166-191.

_____. 1984. "Domesticity and the Denigration of Women." In *Rethinking Women's Roles.* O'Brien and Tiffany, eds., op. cit. pp. 13-31.

Vayda, Andrew P. 1969. "Expansion and Warfare among Swidden Agriculturalists." In *Environment and Cultural Behavior.* Vayda, ed., op. cit. pp. 202-216.

Vayda, Andrew P. and Bonnie McCay. 1975. "New Directions in Ecology and Ecological Anthropology." *Annual Review of Anthropology* 4:293-306.

Veblen, Thorsten. 1953, originally 1899. *The Theory of the Leisure Class: An Economic Study of Institutions.* New York: New American Library.

Venkatachalam, P.S. 1962. *A Study of the Diet, Nutrition, and Health of the People of the Chimbu Area (New Guinea Highlands).* Territory of Papua and New Guinea, Department of Public Health, Monograph No. 4.

Vicedom and Tischner. 1943-1948. *Die Mbowamb: Die Kultur der Hagenberg-Stämme in Östlichen Zentral Neuguinea.* Hamburg: Friederichsen, de Gruyter, and Co.

Waddell, Eric. 1972. *The Mound Builders: Agricultural Practices, Environment, and Society in the Central Highlands of New Guinea.* Seattle: University of Washington Press.

Wagner, Roy. 1974. "Are There Social Groups in the New Guinea Highlands?" In *Frontiers of Anthropology.* Murray J. Leaf, ed. New York: D. Van Nostrand Company. pp. 95-122.

Walter, Michael A.H.B. 1978. "Prudent Lechers: A Further Syndrome for Meggitt's Analysis of Sexual Antagonism in the Highlands of Papua New Guinea." *Bidragen Tot de Taal-, Land-, en Volkenkunde* 134:170-180.

Watson, James B. 1965a. "From Hunting to Horticulture in the New Guinea Highlands." *Ethnology* 4:295-309.

_____. 1965b. "The Significance of a Recent Ecological Change in the Central Highlands of New Guinea." *Journal of the Polynesian Society* 74:438-450.

_____. 1967a. "Horticultural Traditions of the Eastern New Guinea Highlands." *Oceania* 38:81-98.

_____. 1967b. "Tairora: The Politics of Despotism in a Small Society." *Anthropological Forum* 2:53-104.

_____. 1970. "Society as Organized Flow: The Tairora Case." *Southwestern Journal of Anthropology* 26:107-124.

_____. 1977. "Pigs, Fodder, and the Jones Effect in Postipomoean New Guinea." *Ethnology* 16:57-70.

White, Benjamin N.F. 1975. "The Economic Importance of Children in a Javanese Village." In *Population and Social Organization.* Moni Nag, ed. The Hague: Mouton Publishers. pp. 127-146.

Whiting, Beatrice B. 1965. "Sex Identity and Physical Violence: A Comparative Study." *American Anthropologist* 67:123-140.

Whiting, John W.M. 1969. "Effects of Climate on Certain Cultural Practices." In *Environment and Cultural Behavior.* Vayda, ed., op cit. pp. 416-450.

Whiting, John W.M., Richard Kluckhohn, and Albert Anthony. 1958. "The Function of Male Initiation Rites at Puberty." In *Readings in Social Psychology.* E.E. Maccoby, T. Newcomb, and E. Hartley, eds. New York: Holt, Rinehart, and Winston. pp. 359-370.

Whiting, John W.M. and Beatrice P. Whiting. 1975. "Aloofness and Intimacy of Husbands and Wives: A Cross-Cultural Study." *Ethos* 3:183-207.
Whyte, Anne. 1978. "Systems as Perceived: A Discussion of 'Maladaptation in Social Systems.'" In *Evolution of Social Systems*. Friedman and Rowlands, eds., op. cit. pp. 73-78.
Williams, George C. 1966. *Adaptation and Natural Selection: A Critique of Some Current Evolutionary Thought*. Princeton: Princeton University Press.
Williams, Mary. 1984. "The Logical Status of Natural Selection and Other Evolutionary Controversies." In *Conceptual Issues*. Elliot Sober, ed., op. cit. pp. 83-98.
Wilson, Edward O. 1975. *Sociobiology: The New Synthesis*. Cambridge, Mass.: Belknap Press.
Wolfenstein, Martha. 1955. "French Parents Take their Children to the Park." In *Childhood in Contemporary Cultures*. Margaret Mead and Martha Wolfenstein, eds. Chicago: University of Chicago Press. pp. 99-117.
Wood, James W. and Peter E. Smouse. 1982. "A Method of Analyzing Density-Dependent Vital Rates with an Application to the Gainj of Papua New Guinea." *American Journal of Physical Anthropology* 58:403-411.
Wynne-Edwards, V.C. 1965. "Self-Regulating Systems in Populations of Animals." *Science* 147:1543-1548.

Index

Adaptation:
  cultural: analogy to Darwinian and, 126-140; criteria for, 126-128, 135-136, 139-140, 142, 144-145; and selection, 128-130
  Darwinian model of, 125-126
  evolutionary, 126, 133, 137, 143n
  homeostatic, 133-137, 143n
  types of, 134
  unconscious, 108-109, 113n, 138
Adaptation theory(ies), in socio-economic group:
  individual adaptation vs. societal adaptation and, 130-138, 142n-146n
  inheritance and cultural traits and, 131-132
  population regulation and, 130, 137-140
  problems with, 128-140, 157
Adolescence, in New Guinea Highland society, 34-35, 38-39
Antagonism:
  characteristics of, 12
  distribution of characteristics of, 9T-11T
  fear as, 17-24
  in Highlands, 12-13
  hostility as, 24
  psycho-social aspects of, 65-66

Bridewealth payments, 31-33

Carrying capacity, 98-106
  defined, 98
  Hassan's model of, 101-102
  problems with use of, 98-101, 111n
Childhood, relation of to adult personality, 68-71
Competition, and socio-economic structure, 82-84

"Descent dogmas", 54
Distribution of goods, conflict over between men and women, 12, 24, 42n, 50

Exchange, 6-7, 20-21, 26, 31-33, 50, 52, 60n, 87-88, 90n-91n

Formal institutions of authority, lacking, 21, 26, 28, 52, 71-72

Genealogy, shallow, 54
Gerontocratic control, ideology about women and, 17-39

Ideology:
  as form of social control, 23, 25-26, 28-30, 42n, 71, 74-75
  manipulation of, and socio-economic structure, 74-75, 81
  and social processes, discrepancy between, 18n, 40n, 42n, 51, 54-59, 117, 122-123, 150-152
Individual, importance of actions of, 26-27, 72-74, 81-82
Individualism, and socio-economic structure, 28, 71-74, 82
Infanticide, 22
Influence, ways of gaining in

New Guinea Highland
society, 28, 71-72
Initiation ritual, 9T, 11T, 18-19, 35, 38-39, 46n

Labor, contribution to:
by women, 6, 9T, 11T, 19-21, 24, 32, 35, 41n, 88
by men, 6, 19-20, 40n

Maladaptation, defined, 134-135
Marriage, and economic/political relationships, 32-33, 48-49, 52-53
Men, age of:
and association with women, 17-24
in competition for women, 19-21
Men, discrepancy between beliefs of older and younger, 17-19, 28-30, 39, 151
Men, young, control over, 26-39
economic, 30-33
political, 30-33

New Guinea Highland(s):
as culture area, 5-9, 14n; area defined, 5-6
differences between Eastern and Western, 7-8, 14n, 38
reasons for study of, 3-4
religion in, 27-28, 43n-44n
societies of, 5-8
New Guinea Highland society:
compared to American society, 154-156
patrilineality of, 50-51
shifting composition of personnel in, 51-58; patterns of marriage and, 52-53; recruitment to local group and, 51-52
structural stresses among men in, 57-59

Patrilineality:
"descent dogmas" in, 54
fictional agnation and, 54, 56, 61n
of New Guinea Highland society, 7, 44n, 50-51, 54
Personality:
competition and, 82-84
complementarity of, defined, 67
ideological manipulation and, 74-75, 81
and individualism, 72-74, 81-82
modal, defined, 63-64
prestige and, 81, 84-89
and society, problems in theory of, 64-66, 68-70, 89n
and socio-economic structure, 63-89
and unconscious as intervening variable in theory of, 68-71
Personality characteristics, defined, 63-64
Personality of adult, relation of to childhood, 68-71
Personality of Highland men:
socio-economic constraint(s) and, 68, 71-89
and socio-economic structure, 66-89, 154-155
Personality of women, 67
Polygyny, 21-22
Population control, development of, 102, 104-106
Population pressure:
in New Guinea Highlands, 95-110

Index

problems in assessing, 97-100, 103-104
Population regulation:
  aversion toward women and, 93-94, 107-110, 115-120
  and adaptation theory(ies), in socio-economic group, 137-140
  as adaptation to environmental constraints, 137-140
  problems in theory of, 102, 107-108, 113n, 135, 137-139, 156-157
Prestige:
  and personality, 81, 84-89
  and socio-economic structure, 6, 32, 81, 84-89, 90n-91n

Reproduction rate:
  physiological factors affecting, 115-116, 140n
  socio-economic factors affecting, 116-120, 140n
  women's influence on, 118-120, 141n

Sexes, relationship between:
  Sanday's theory concerning ecological variables and, 121-124; problems with, 122-124
  social matrix of, 47-59, 139
Social alignment, importance of fluidity of in socio-economic structure, 26-27, 50-53, 71-73, 85, 152-153
Social structure:
  dissimilarity of women's and men's relationships in, 47-50
  non-alignment of women and, 47-50
Socio-economic constraint(s), and personality of Highland men, 71-89
Socio-economic structure:
  competition and, 82-84
  ideological manipulation and, 23, 26, 28-30, 74-75, 81
  "ideologized" version of in New Guinea Highland society, 150-152
  importance of fluidity of social alignment in, 26-27, 50-53, 71-73, 85, 152-153
  individualism and, 28, 71-74, 82
  personality of Highland men and, 63-89
  prestige and, 6, 32, 81, 84-89, 90n-91n
Solidarity, male, 55-57, 61n
  and devaluation of women, 55-56
Suicide by women, 9T, 11T, 12, 43n

Unconscious, as intervening variable in theory of personality, 69-71

Violence toward women:
  in New Guinea Highlands, 12, 25-26, 85-86
  in U.S.A., 13n-14n

Warfare, 33, 48-49, 51, 53, 55, 58, 60n, 81-82, 91n, 120, 144n, 146n-147n
Women in New Guinea Highlands:
  aversion toward: adaptive significance of, 108-109; effectiveness of as population regulator, 117-118, 120; and

population regulation, 93-94, 107-110, 115-120
age of men, and association with, 17-24
control over, importance of, 21, 24, 29, 88
non-alignment of into corporate group, 47-50
personality characteristics of, 67
scarcity of, 21-23
as source of pollution, 1-2, 9T, 11T, 93-94
as source of productive labor, 6, 9T, 11T, 19-21, 24, 32, 35, 41n, 88
violence toward, 12, 25-26, 85-86